AFRICAN LEADERS'
TÊTE À TÊTE

Navigating Entity Design And Prioritization For Systemic Outcomes

AFRICAN LEADERS' TÊTE À TÊTE

Navigating Entity Design And Prioritization For Systemic Outcomes

DR. LUCY S. NEWMAN

FOREWORD BY AMB. OMBENI SEFUE

PYXIDIA HOUSE PUBLISHERS

AFRICAN LEADERS' TÊTE À TÊTE:
Navigating Entity Design And Prioritization
For Systemic Outcomes
Copyright©2022 by Dr. Lucy S. Newman

Request for information on this title should be addressed to
Dr. Lucy S. Newman
Email: lucy@drlsnewman.com
+234 805 605 0000

Library of Congress Cataloging-in-Publication Data

Dr. Lucy S. Newman
AFRICAN LEADERS' TÊTE À TÊTE:
Navigating Entity Design And Prioritization
For Systemic Outcomes
ISBN-13: 978-1-946530-35-6 (Paperback)
ISBN-10: 1-946530-35-2 (Paperback)
1. Leadership - Consulting - Non-fiction 1. Title
Library of Congress Control Number: 2022947133

Edited by Winnie Aduayi

Published in Dallas Texas by Pyxidia House Publishers. A registered trademark of Pyxidia Concept llc. www.pyxidiahouse.com
info@pyxidiahouse.com

Printed in the United States of America

To family. History records indicate that Africa is our first home as human beings. So, humanity has been African from the beginning. Covid-19 Pandemic takes it a notch higher and reminds us that when the chips are down, we are one family – the entire human race.

I am a product of a multi-layered web of nuclear, extended, tribal, professional, and social connections that transcend gender, tribe, race, religion, social class, and location, nurtured by divine orchestrations. Thus, in the spirit of the lyrics of the African Union's anthem and the ancient African philosophy of *Ubuntu*, meaning humanity to others, and interpreted as *"I am what I am because of who we all are"*, this book is to you as family.

ACKNOWLEDGEMENTS

In Africa, we have a saying that *"it takes a village to raise a child"*. This saying certainly held true with this publication! It took the support of many people playing various inspiring roles to see this project through. I am profoundly grateful to all and would like to particularly acknowledge the following persons and their major roles in this publication journey.

I am profoundly grateful to my publisher, Pyxidia House, for accepting to publish the manuscript and nominating the following persons to play various roles from contracting to developmental editing, proofing, securing listings and copyright registrations, layout and design, digital conversion, and publication. Thank you so much, Winnie Aduayi, Craig Smith, Samantha Hughes, Okiemute Somuvie, Oscar Brent, Rick Simmons, and Josh Pritchard. You all contributed to turning the manuscript into the wonderful book that is now available to all. What a delightful experience it has been working with all of you.

I appreciate everyone who showed such great enthusiasm for this work and the time invested in reading the manuscript, being sounding boards and giving feedback from a neutral position on the subject. I recognize the time invested in doing this and the need to keep the confidence required.

Thank you so much, Ambassador Ombeni Sefue, for writing the foreword; your experience and background as a diplomat and an African leader, who has continued to engage African leaders and heads of governments in Africa's trajectory through the years, is a blessing.

My dear brother, Idonesit, God bless you for your feedback as a well-travelled and highly networked African diasporan.

My dear friend and husband, Dr Rotimi Gabriel Olokodana, what a blessing you are to the family and me. Thank you for not only reviewing the manuscript and providing feedback but also managing the home front when I had to hunker down to complete the manuscript.

What can I say about my children? Samson, Solomon, and Noble, what a blessing it is to be your mother and a beneficiary of your love, support, and feedback through my career journey, especially this book project. Our beautiful Esther, God bless you. May God continue to bless and nurture each and all of you into your destined places.

Thank you all.

CONTENTS

Author Note

African Leaders' Tête À Tête is a discussion between the author and three main spheres of leadership with impact in Africa, which include: [a] Individual leaders with aspiration for self-application of principles to address personal or expected professional growth as an individual. [b] Corporate leaders with primary, secondary, or tertiary responsibility for entities that include corporate organizations, institutions, government ministries, departments, and agencies. [c] Leaders with jurisdictional and jurisdictional cluster leadership responsibilities.

The book is designed to provide a safe environment to undertake personal journeys and, therein, support the leader in navigating the dual issues of how to derive wholesome entities that facilitate the emergence of mega outcomes and chart pathways to making choices among competing strategic options. We now live in a very dynamic global system that is learning the art of navigating continuity despite sudden systemic disruptions similar to the challenges posed by the COVID-19 Pandemic, security upheavals, and other situations that threaten the continuity of our ways of living and operating. Business models are mutating; there are re-alignments in strategic alliances, including stakeholder engagements, that offer opportunities to modernize and re-organize as individuals, organizations, jurisdictions, and jurisdictional clusters. More so, demographics are also changing, especially in Africa.

Since the intention is to enable the reader to have a perception of a one-on-one private conversation with the author, *African Leaders' Tête À Tête: Navigating Entity Design And Prioritization For Systemic Outcomes* is presented as a compact, highly simplified presentation of concepts, using a storytelling and conversational format. It is a book for extremely busy people who simply want to get the essence and implement it. Therefore, the book is presented in five parts, preceded by an introductory section. Part One, titled, *The Lion's Gaze*, gives an overview of all key concepts discussed in the book within the context of Africa as a continent and opportunities there-in, as well as the two concepts – ED4SP© and SWOTPlus©. Part Two highlights how the two concepts can apply to the leader as an individual, and it's rightly titled, *The Leader*. Part Three provides highlights of how the key concepts can be applied to an organization or cluster of similar organizations, as applicable to industries and sectors – it is titled, *The Organization*. Part Four, titled, *The Jurisdictions*, provides highlights of how the two concepts can be adapted to a jurisdiction or a cluster of jurisdictions in similar or neighbouring locations. Part Five is the concluding Part, and it is technically a call to action, as applicable to the Leader, Organizations, and Jurisdictions. It is aptly titled, *The Momentum*.

To get the best out of the book, I kindly suggest you read Parts One and Two at once to grasp the key issues. Then, depending on your situation as a leader of an organizational entity or cluster of organizational entities, as with an Industry or Sector, you may proceed to Part Three and thereafter jump to the final section, Part Five. However, if you are a leader of a jurisdiction or jurisdictional cluster, or leader of an entity with oversight of a region, sub-region or continent, kindly read Parts One and Two, then proceed to Part Four and Part Five, respectively. My personal preference, however, is that whatever your leadership status, you will read through the whole of the *African Leaders' Tête À Tête* with at least a fleeting glance at even the Part that doesn't address your present leadership positioning. Knowledge of applying the concepts in all spheres will likely position you more for a truly systemic outcome. This way, a fast reader should be done in about four hours or less, including making self-reflection notes.

I look forward to hearing from you regarding thoughts on the issues raised, experience in implementing the ideas discussed, and any requests resulting from decisions on any of the propositions. I am just an email away and look forward to hearing from you in continuation of this conversation.

FOREWORD

This erudite, unique, and immensely outstanding book by Dr. Lucy Surhyel Newman on transformational leadership in Africa gets to the heart of the deepest passions and aspirations for the African continent to be economically free and secure. Dr. Lucy Surhyel Newman was a trusted consultant and advisor to me in 2021 when I led an African Peer Review mission to Namibia to assess critical aspects of leadership and governance in that country.

I was on the Panel of Eminent Persons of the African Peer Review Mechanism for five years, and during that time, we conducted many assessments of governance in Africa and worked with many advisors and consultants; in my view, Dr. Newman was among the best. I was, therefore, not surprised that shortly after the completion of the Namibia mission, Dr. Newman was invited to play a similar role on a South Africa mission.

I have experienced first-hand governance challenges,

especially of a transformational nature, having worked as a personal assistant to two presidents of Tanzania during a period of far-reaching political and economic reforms; I also served as Ambassador to Canada and the United States and as Permanent Representative of Tanzania to the United Nations in New York. Within the country, I rose to be Secretary to the Cabinet and Head of Public Service. So, I know much about the challenges of transformational leadership in Africa; thus, I welcome this book and recommend it to readers.

In my current position as Chair of the Board of Directors of the Institute of African Leadership for Sustainable Development, popularly known in Tanzania as Uongozi Institute, I am always uncomfortable seeing that many of the books we use to build the capacity of African leaders are not written by Africans. Thus, Dr Newman's book is a welcome experience that will definitely find a place of pride on our bookshelves.

Dr. Lucy Newman is a performance improvement and corporate governance specialist, and her passion for transformational leadership, especially in Africa, was evident during the mission to Namibia, as was her knowledge and competence in this space. The qualities I saw in her have emerged in this book. I applaud Dr. Newman's storytelling style, which makes the book readable and practical. It should appeal to all kinds of readers, in the continent and those in the Diaspora.

The paradox she raises of Africa being so richly endowed, yet relatively so poor needs renewed attention. This rich endowment and the strategic position of Africa in the global space precipitated the "scramble" for Africa in the late 19th Century. Despite the exploitation – looting, even of those resources, many still remain. And the sad thing is that until now, most of those resources have not been utilised appropriately to create a more prosperous Africa.

The underutilisation of our resources has been brought to sharp focus by the Ukraine war, which has created a huge shortage of wheat in Africa because we depend so much on wheat from Ukraine and Russia, even when Africa has the vast agricultural lands and climate to feed itself and quite a bit of the world as well.

It is sad that the African Union, other than contributing to the independence and liberation of African countries, has not realised the vision of its founding fathers - dreams of economic integration and political unity. Africa remains divided, thus, making it weak and vulnerable in the face of a new scramble for our continent. Today, African countries further enable this new scramble as we continue to trade more with the outside world than with each other.

We need to get our priorities right, unlocking the potential of our people and resources in our own continent if we must achieve Agenda 2063 – *"The Africa We Want"*. Priorities must have strategic plans – short, medium, and long-term plans, and also the political will to focus on them for the long haul. We must adopt the attitude of perseverance, or as Dr. Newman calls it, momentum– not changing course every time there is a change of leadership is key.

I am glad Dr. Newman raises the issue of inclusive and sustainable development – a development that doesn't leave some of our people behind. The level of income inequality in our continent is unacceptably high, coupled with unacceptably high levels of youth unemployment and desperation, which poses significant risks to political stability.

The extraction of our natural resources and agricultural production must create jobs and incomes for our countries through their value chain and local content. The era of exporting raw materials must end now, and trade among African countries must pick up. AfCFTA must not fail.

The book has been informed and enriched by Dr. Newman's broad experience across the continent and the many engagements, interactions, and discussions she has had over the years with leaders and citizens, stakeholders, and experts. I commend the book for simplifying complex themes and providing easily understood guidance for leaders who want to be part of a strategic transformational journey that will catapult Africa to the space it should occupy on the global stage. The focus on self-analysis to identify strengths, weaknesses, and risks is welcome and critical, whether as an individual, an organisation, or a country.

African Leaders' Tête À Tête: Navigating Entity Design And Prioritization For Systemic Outcomes is more than a book; it is a manual to help leaders of government, institutions, and corporations provide transformational leadership. I commend Dr. Newman for writing such a needed book – an erudite body of work by an African scholar. That a book of such significance and relevance to African leadership and governance is written by an African must be applauded by people like me, who believe in African scholarship serving Africa.

In recommending this book to readers, I urge more African scholars to do likewise because it is sad that so many years after our countries became independent, so many books on our continent are still written by non-Africans. We can and must act now to redress this sad situation.

Ambassador Ombeni Sefue
Chairperson
Institute of African Leadership for Sustainable Development [Uongozi Institute], Tanzania.

PREFACE

"Leaders don't move mountains with mountains of data. They do it by giving their audiences a piece of their heart" – **Carmine Gallo, 2016.**

Diamonds & Kotler (2012), in the book, <u>Abundance: The Future Is Better Than You Think</u>, said, *"humanity is now entering a period of radical transformation in which technology has the potential to significantly raise the basic standards of living for every [person] on the planet. Within a generation, we will be able to provide goods and services once reserved for the wealthy few to all who need them or desire them. Abundance for all is actually within our grasp".* The *African Leaders' Tête À Tête* is a one-on-one discussion between the reader and author. The focus is on Africa as a continent in transformation and possible ways that we can participate in this transformation for systemic impact in Africa, irrespective of where we live or work. We will discuss issues personal to a leader – what the leader needs to consider in positioning to effectively contribute as an individual, as a leader in an organization, as an individual leading an organization or cluster of organizations, or as a leader of jurisdiction or cluster of jurisdictions in Africa. In my discussions with many African leaders in the diaspora, I observed that many want to contribute to Africa's development but have challenges knowing how to and in what format. I have also interacted with leaders of foreign private companies operating in Africa who want to make a socio-economic impact but worry about the accuracy of their perception of where help is needed in their host communities because some of their presumed apt support projects end up failing and become unsustainable.

The African diaspora community is a vital stakeholder in Africa's transformation, and many African leaders recognize this emerging fact. Kajunju (2013), in a special submission to CNN titled, Africa's Secret Weapon: The Diaspora, reported that the African Union Commission broadly defines the African diaspora as "*peoples of African origin living outside the continent, irrespective of their citizenship and nationality and who are willing to contribute to the development of the continent and the building of the African Union.*" The report further indicated that by leveraging the skills, ingenuity, and resources of the African Diaspora, diasporans are uniquely positioned to contribute to boosting economic growth and prosperity in Africa. Now, almost a decade after this submission, this is even more obvious!

In response to this, many African diaspora networks with a

specific focus on jurisdictions or cultural clusters have tried to fill this gap via information platforms and engagements. Leaders working and living in Africa or affiliated with organizations with business interests in Africa are the front line in the transformation journey. I believe that the Middle East, Asia, and Africa corridor is the new global frontier. Developments since the onset of the COVID-19 Pandemic have also affirmed this. Africa remains at the center of many concerns, having diverse jurisdictions that are distinct in nature, positioning, and endowment. For reasons of sub-optimal leverage and alliance systems as well as differing degrees of human and institutional capacity, many jurisdictions in Africa have remained countries of potential. Because of these sovereign constraints, entities within have continued to be so impacted. However, there has been a shift in many issues over the past decade. Africa and Africans have aspirations for the continent and the people of Africa. Africans are also beginning to talk to one another on collective pathways into the future. Thus, Agenda 2063 – *the Africa we want.*

Diamonds & Kotler (2012), in the book, <u>Abundance: The Future Is Better Than You Think</u>, defined abundance as *"a big vision compressed into a small-time frame".* They further explained that the *"next twenty-five years could remake the world, but this won't happen on its own. There are plenty of issues to be faced, not all of them technological in nature. Overcoming the psychological blocks – cynicism, pessimism, and all those other crutches of contemporary thinking that keep many of us from believing in the possibility of abundance is just as important. To accomplish this, we need to understand the way our brain shapes our beliefs, and our beliefs shape our reality".* From another perspective, the concept of leadership continues to be as intriguing as it has been from primitive times to the modern day. For this reason, I would like to use a classic reference on the subject. A classic book that I have found precious and timeless through the years is Bass & Stogdill's (1990) <u>Handbook of Leadership: Theory, Research & Managerial Applications</u>. The quotes include:

"Leadership definitions indicate a progression of thought, although historically, many trends overlapped. The earlier definitions identified leadership as a focus of group process and movement, personality in action. The next type considered it as the art of inducing compliance. The more recent definitions conceive leadership in terms of influence relationships, power differentials, persuasion, influence on goal achievement, role differentiation, reinforcement, initiation of structure and perceived attributions of behavior that are consistent with what the perceivers believe leadership to be. Leadership may involve all of these."

"Transformational leaders were categorized as intellectual leaders, leaders of reform or revolution, and heroes or idealogues" *...it is the transformational leader who raises consciousness (about higher considerations) through articulation and role modeling. Through transformational leaders, levels of aspiration are raised, legitimated, and turned into political demands."*

The African Leaders' Tête À Tête is a discussion that will explore the African Leaders' consideration of ways to attain systemic outcomes that can pave the way for tangible contributions to the search for abundance in Africa's emerging transformation. We will explore this through the lens of self-aware leaders' practical application of two concepts I developed over the years and copyrighted in 2021. Systems thinking, transformational leadership mindset and continued performance improvement based on life learning orientation are important to this discussion. Hence, there is a provision for the reader to make notes within the book.

Why the *African Leaders' Tête À Tête?*

"To sum up, Mega thinking and planning is about defining a shared success, achieving it, and being able to prove it. It is not a focus on one's organization alone but a focus on society now and in the future. It is about adding value to all stakeholders. It is responsible, responsive, and ethical value add for all." – **Roger Kaufman, 2006.**

The continent of Africa presents a paradox of a sort. It is so richly endowed, yet so poor, relative to its level of natural endowment. However, there are shifts of monumental dimensions emerging. There is increasing interest in the continent and its people. I love Africa and make no mistake in making that known everywhere, even as I consider myself a global citizen and life student of nature. The general observation is that this feeling is popular within the diaspora community and self-aware African leaders with increasing intensity, especially in the past decade. Africa is emerging; therefore, the big question for context is, "what happened in the past decade to trigger this interest in Africa?" I think I know one factor – Agenda 2063: *the Africa we want.* The world is awaiting the blossoming of this beautiful continent.

Therefore, this book is a conversation about individual leadership journeys in search of how to make systemic contributions as individual entities, organizational entities or clusters, jurisdictional entities, or jurisdictional clusters. *African Leaders' Tête À Tête* is a one-on-one discussion between the reader and the author. The intention is to present a book that makes the reader feels as if it is not literarily reading a book but sitting next to the author and having a discussion while on an intercontinental flight, a long train ride, or a road trip. The intention is to have the reader reflect on the concepts discussed and then plan what to do with the information shared and questions triggered. The reason for this writing style is because I have, over the course of my almost three and half decades of work experience, worked closely with leaders and from these engagements, as well as watching highly effective leaders up close, I have come to recognize that most leaders would really like simplified practical ideas that can be viewed end-to-end at once and if there is any aspiration for more detail on any aspect, they can infer or make applicable findings.

Some of the questions I have been asked by many leaders

over the latter two decades of my career, as I have had the privilege of engaging various leaders, include:

[a] How can one put all aspects of my organization in a compressed and simplified manner to show balance?

[b] Is the issue of resource limitation always the matter with strategic initiatives?

[c] How do I quickly prioritize and allocate resources to competing strategic initiatives?

[d] I will not be in my role endlessly, so how can I make a meaningful contribution with systemic outcomes?

The reality is that unless a leader has an opportunity to establish and draw on objective mentors or executive coaches, the challenge of finding the time and the person to have these one-on-one conversations are rare due to time constraints of the leader and the breadth and depth of knowledge and experience of leader's chosen coach. Such conversations also require immense vulnerability on the part of the leader. As the saying goes, *"it is lonely at the top"*. Moreso, the general erroneous expectation is that the leader has all the answers! The reality, however, is that many highly effective leaders are life learners who learn on the go within limited time constraints to deliver mega outcomes. This is partly why I decided to write the *African Leaders' Tête À Tête* at this milestone in my career and at this particular time in Africa's trajectory on the global world stage.

The perspectives I will be sharing will derive from almost

three and a half decades of cross-industry working experiences in staff roles from entry-level to C-Suit, as a counterpart staff on consulting projects as well as external consultancies, board memberships and policy advisory. I have had the privilege of cross-jurisdictional collaborations and projects that include some of my former employers' partners with locations in the United States, Africa, Asia, and the Middle East. In my life learning journey, I have also learned much from serving on boards, jury panels and Think Tanks, leading the design and delivery of executive to board director capacity-building interventions. Apart from case-based studies at the University of Phoenix and INSEAD, I have particularly found side discussions at professional networks, conferences, seminars, and client strategic retreats profoundly inspiring and offering deep insights into issues, which have immensely helped in my zeal for customized solutions to clients. I have continued to observe the criticality of context setting in every intervention, whether on a micro institution-specific and macro sectoral or jurisdictional basis based on applicable policies. From these exposures, I have come to understand the multiplier effect of having leaders who are well informed, innately inspired, and focused on positively taking control of their points of contribution to make an impact, build high-performing entities, and lead collaboratively while being active and value-adding stakeholders in their space – be it an organization, a government ministry, department, agency, or a political office in the national, sub-regional, and even continental space.

The firm conviction that inspired me and contributed much to this book is that when entities thrive, jobs are created, taxes are paid, and services are procured. When jobs are created, families are impacted in terms of health, education, and welfare, with multipliers. When jurisdictions are well run and governed, the human development index gets a higher chance of improving, and per capita investment in the citizens and residents gets a chance at improving. When sub-regions run effectively, neighbouring jurisdictions share experiences via the sub-regional blocks and collaboratively seek progress. While these projections may come across as overly idealistic, this is what inspired me to write *African Leaders' Tête À Tête: Navigating Entity Design And Prioritization For Systemic Outcomes*, using storytelling format and as a conversation between the leader and the author in a compacted and very simplified manner. My hope is that like Gallo [2016] said, I would not have used data to move mountains but move mountains by giving the reader a piece of my heart as a global citizen that is proudly African and wants to see as many readers as possible contribute to and possibly share in this African transformation as it unfolds.

PART ONE
The Lion's Gaze

"Tibetan Buddhist monks excel at concentration. They tell a traditional tale about focus called 'The Lion's Gaze', which says; when you throw a ball to a dog, it chases the ball. But when you throw a ball to a lion, it keeps its gaze on you. When we tell a story, our lion's gaze is one thing – connecting with our audience" – **Murray Nossel** (2018).

As with every accomplishment that is worthwhile in life, the outcome derives from a decision to commit and focus. Real learning and growth occur when we push the boundaries of our current habits, experiences, and understandings. That's where we are compelled to consider and adopt thoughtful ways of engaging with others, understanding ourselves, the cultures, and the environment wherein we operate. This form of intelligent learning represents the high point of human potential and is often the source of the most outstanding achievements in history. It is not taught in our schools nor analyzed by professors; it often comes as a result of focused attention. This intense focus sparks all kinds of ideas, and when allowed to take its course in time, something remarkable begins to take shape. As we observe, learn, and follow the lead, we gain clarity, learn the rules, and understand how things work and fit together, and as we keep practising, we gain mastery, allowing us to begin to see connections that we would ordinarily not see.

Leadership or strategy implementation are very broad concepts that have been documented through the years and continue to generate interest, especially at very dynamic times, as seen over the last decade and still emerging. Firstly, the lion's gaze of this conversation will apply to Africa and the reader as a contributor to the possible outcomes based on the reader's application of insights that will be discussed. Secondly, I will be assuming that the conversation is between myself and the individual. Africans in Africa and the diaspora, as well as persons with strong passion or aspirations, to support the continent within a particular sector, country, or the entire continent, are welcome to this conversation.

In terms of spheres of application of our discussion, there will be three spheres. Firstly, the individual leader; secondly, the organizational or institutional leader sphere, which will also recognize the possibility of the reader being a leader of a cluster of organizations in terms of agencies of a ministry, sector, or industry. The third sphere is jurisdictional or a cluster of jurisdictions in terms of subregional or continental context. You and I are, first of all, individuals and have our individual entity as a person in existence, as a unit in humanity; thus, the *Individual Leader*. Based on these views, you and I operate at different levels as a leader within a team or a functional unit within the nuclear family, the extended family, a neighbourhood, social or professional network, and by residency as diaspora or native. We will address these dimensions in the *Individual Leader* sphere in Part Two. Depending on our present or aspired career life cycle stage, you and I may also be a small business owner, running a multigenerational family business, a team member or team leader within a functional area at work, or leading an organization, institution, ministry, or department in government. You may also be reading this book because you lead a cluster of organizations within an industry or sector. We will address these dimensions in the *Organizational Leader* sphere in Part Three. Then, in Part Four, the final spere will address jurisdictional, subregional, or continental issues applicable to navigating entity design and prioritization for mega outcomes. Part Five is *The Momentum*, which is generally a call to action.

In summary, Part One of *African Leaders' Tête À Tête*, which is aptly titled "The Lions' Gaze", will provide a high-level overview of Africa and its alignment issues as applicable to its being a paradox of a sort. Part One concludes with a high-level introduction to two concepts that I have used over the years, which are now copyrighted and presented here; these include:
[1] Entity Design for Sustainable Performance [ED4SP©].
[2] Entity Implementation within SWOTPlus©.

Parts Two, Three, and Four will create the space for us to discuss how these concepts can be applied to an Individual Leader in Part Two, as an Organizational and Institutional Leader in Part Three, or to Jurisdictional Leader in Part Four. Then, Part Five is *The Momentum*, which will provide reflection opportunities to consider the adoption of the concepts in contributing to Africa's aspired and emerging transformation.

I

Africa – The Paradox In Transformation

In discussing Africa as a paradox in transformation and the momentum required in *African Leaders' Tête À Tête*, I would like to reference some sections of Newman (November, 2021) being a paper that I presented at the Second Virtual Symposium on "Economics of Ignorance", a program of Hale Associates Centre. My presentation as referenced, was titled, Africa's Current Status: The Required Alignment.

Africa At First Glance

Paradoxically, despite its many woes and violence, Africa has become a beacon of hope and is returning as a subject of history, considering its favourable demographic profile and economic and social progress in recent times. With over one billion inhabitants, representing 18 percent of the world's population, Africa is regaining the place it once occupied at the beginning of the 16th century – a rich and thriving continent. According to Wikipedia, Africa is the world's second largest and second most populous continent, after Asia, in both cases. It is about 30.3 million km2 (11.7 million square miles), including adjacent islands; it covers six percent of Earth's total surface area and 20 percent of its land area. In terms of location, the continent straddles the equator and the prime meridian, making it the only continent in the world to be situated in all four cardinal hemispheres. It is the only continent to stretch from the northern temperate to the southern temperate zones. Time zones UTC-1 to UTC +4. The continent is surrounded by the Mediterranean Sea to the north, the Isthmus of Suez and the Red Sea to the northeast, the Indian Ocean to the southeast and the Atlantic Ocean to the west.

I have often found myself explaining to some westerners that Africa is NOT a Country as they tend to assume. Wikipedia reports that it is a continent of 54 fully recognized sovereign states (countries), eight territories, and two de facto independent states with limited or no recognition. In terms of human history, Africa is considered the oldest inhabited territory on earth, given historical records that indicate the human species originated from the continent. At about 3300 BC, the historical record opens in Northern Africa with the rise of literacy in the Pharaonic civilization of Ancient Egypt. The pyramids of Egypt are evidence of such mathematical and structural design ingenuity. Algeria is Africa's largest country by area, and Nigeria is its largest by population.

African nations cooperate through the establishment of the African Union (AU), a continental union consisting of 55 member states. The AU was announced in the Sirte Declaration in Sirte, Libya, on 9 September 1999, calling for the establishment of the African Union, founded on 26 May 2001 in Addis Ababa. Africa has five regions with five sub-regional bodies within the African Union, applicable to North Africa, East Africa, West Africa, Central Africa, and Southern Africa. One major factor about Africa is the historical influence of Europe, as indicated by the colonial ties of some African countries to Belgian, Britain, France, Italy, Portugal, Spain, and others. The Arabian influence also has the Maghreb or Arab-speaking Africa. In view of this diversity, Africa is a continent with a very high linguistic and cultural diversity, estimated at 1500-2000 unique African languages.

In terms of population, Worldometer reports that the total global population as of 8 July 2022 is 7.96 billion, while Africa's population as of then was 1.41 billion. That is about 17.7 percent of the total world population, with the median age being 20. The recorded annual growth rate is 2.49 percent, and the fertility rate is 4.4 percent, with a population density of 45 per km^2. Africa is demographically the youngest continent – the World Economic Forum reports that the world's youngest countries are all in Africa. Out of the 20 youngest countries by demography in the world, 19 are in

Africa. One major factor that I would like us to note as applicable to the aspirations of this discussion in the *African Leaders' Tête À Tête* is that this African population credential can be both a strength and a great risk if taken in the context of unemployment rates, literacy levels, quality of life, socio-political unrest, and resilience of the various jurisdictions. Therefore, worthy for us to note in terms of the risk for the continent.

A recent development that has profound potential for redirecting the fortunes of Africa is "Agenda 2063: *The Africa We Want*". It is Africa's blueprint and master plan for transforming Africa into a global powerhouse, using a 50-year vision for the period 2013 to 2063, subdivided into five ten-year segments. Its goals include inclusive and sustainable development via a pan-African drive for unity, self-determination, freedom, progress, and collective prosperity pursued under Pan-Africanism and African Renaissance. Many initiatives emanating from Agenda 2063 includes the African Continental Free Trade Area (AfCFTA), a free trade area founded in 2018, with trade effective in 2021. It was created by the African Continental Free Trade Agreement among 54 of the 55 African Union nations, thus, creating the world's largest free-trade area since the establishment of the World Trade Organisation in 1995. The AfCFTA could increase the value of intra-African trade by 15 – 25 percent by 2040 and boost economic output by $29 trillion by 2050. The AfCFTA is one of the flagship projects of the First Ten-Year Implementation Plan (2014

-2023) under the AU's "Agenda 2063 – *The Africa We Want*".

The general perception before Agenda 2063 is that Africa has a culture of sub-optimal commitment to medium to long-term interventions and projects. The dynamism in the political space, short-termism culture, and high tension within the private and public sectors in most jurisdictions of the African continent, tended not to appreciate the three to five years average gestation required for systemic impact. This is so unlike the approach in Asia, where for instance, the People's Republic of China has the two centenaries term, which refers to two 100-year anniversaries and a stated set of economic and political goals based on a 100-year plan that is intentionally followed across a generation of leaders and around which the people unite.

African Leaders' Tête À Tête being released just before the end of Agenda 2023's first ten-year block from 2014 to 2023 is a deliberate action to get you and I aligned on how we can contribute to the next ten-year block from 2023, all being well. I hope this discussion turns out to be mutually inspiring, given our shared keen interest in Africa.

Africa, A Worrisome Paradox Of Wealth And Poverty

Africa is a resource-rich continent – recent growth in commodities, services, and manufacturing sales has indicated this reality. According to the World Economic Forum, six of the world's ten fastest-growing economies are in Africa. PWC reported that in recent years, Africa's average annual GDP growth has consistently outpaced the global average and is expected to remain at least six percent until 2023. The World Bank's GDP growth (annual percentage) for the world was 2.562 pecent in 2019 and now plummeted to -3.405 percent for 2020 due to factors including covid-19, security, and climate change. The World Bank predicts that Sub-Saharan Africa alone will be home to more than one billion people, half of whom will be under 25 years old by 2050.

Africa is also technically the poorest continent – DevelopmentAid reported that in 2021 there were 490 million people in Africa living in extreme poverty, or 36 percent of the total population. The United Nations projects that 514 million Africans risk falling below the extreme poverty line in 2021 due to COVID-19. If we add the impact of security challenges and climate change, then systemic risks can increase. Africa's Nominal Per Capital GDP for 2021 estimate was $1,860, while the world average was $11,570. Technically this makes Africa the poorest inhabited continent in the world, rated number six out of the seven contents, ahead of only Antarctica, the southernmost continent and the site of the South Pole, which is virtually uninhabited, being an ice-covered landmass. In March 2013, Africa was identified as the world's poorest inhabited continent; however, the World

Bank expects that most African countries will reach "middle income" status (defined as at least US$1,000 per person a year) by 2025 if the growth rate continues. According to the African Center for Economic Transformation [ACET], the AfCFTA may be the last opportunity for Africa's Economic Transformation! AfCFTA has also been predicted to transform multilateral relationship arrangements within Africa and the flow of Foreign Direct Investments into and out of Africa. Yes, OUT OF Africa!

In the next two chapters, we will review the two concepts that you and I will be using as tools on this journey of discussion, thereby wrapping up part one of *African Leaders' Tête À Tête*. On this note, I would like to reference another Management Classic, Wren's (1994) Evolutions of Management, as cited in Newman (2008), which said, "within the practices of the past, are lessons of history for tomorrow; a flow of events and ideas that link yesterday, today, and tomorrow in a continuous stream. People occupy but one point in this stream of time and can see the distant past with a high degree of clarity; however, as we approach the present, our perspective becomes less clear. The future must be a projection and a tenuous one at best. New ideas, subtle shifts in themes, and emerging environmental events all bring new directions to evolving management thought". The first of the five ten-year blocks of the Agenda 2063 Master Plan (2014 – 2023) expires in 2023. Thus, the question is, what will be our role in the next ten-year block from 2023?

The year 2023 also happens to be an intensely political year for Africa due to the general elections in Nigeria, Sierra Leone, Zimbabwe, Liberia, South Sudan, The Dominican Republic of Congo, and Swazi. Other elections include Gambia - local elections, Mauritania - parliamentary elections, and Malagasy - presidential elections. Kenya just concluded its presentational and parliamentary elections in August 2022, with outcomes that may require national discussions into 2023. The year 2023 is, therefore, critical to most of Africa and will likely have implications for many planning scenarios in Africa.

African Leaders' Tête À Tête is a small contribution to the discussion on how individuals as leaders living in Africa interested in participating in this emerging African transformation journey can meaningfully participate, thereby making systemic contributions in ways that matter. That is why I started Chapter One with an overview of Africa at first glance and Africa being a paradox of wealth and poverty. My discussion with you is a journey to the Africa We Want. Therefore, this discussion moves beyond the conventional view when examining poverty and wealth in Africa, which places greater emphasis on the "why" of Africa's failures rather than on the solutions to finding the Africa we want.

2

ED4SP©

I created the acronym ED4SP© to enable "Entity Design for Sustainable Performance". Design for sustainability goes beyond the average expected life of a product or service, and anything being developed must consider the well-being of future generations so that their needs are not sacrificed. Thus, the term design for sustainable performance is generally related to sustainability and sustainable development. According to Vallero & Brasier, 2008, "sustainability considers people's current needs without compromising future generations' ability to fulfil their needs". Over the years, attempts have been made to appreciate, understand, and implement the concept of entity design for sustainability.

Thus, ED4SP© is presented here as a schematic for the sustainable performance of an entity. The term "entity" in *African Leaders' Tête À Tête* applies to individual leader[s], organization[s], or jurisdiction[s]. ED4SP© hinges on general systems thinking; as a result, I would like to leverage a classic literature, Ludwig von Bertalanffy's (1972) "General Systems Theory", which took a holistic view and defined a system as *"a set of elements standing in interrelation among themselves and the environment"*.

Design for sustainability seeks to reduce negative impacts on the environment and the entity's health, thereby improving development performance. The primary objectives of sustainability are to reduce the consumption of non-renewable resources, minimize waste, and create productive environments. And the basic principles of design for sustainable performance include the entity's ability to optimize the potential and improve operational and maintenance practices. Using a sustainable design philosophy encourages decisions at each phase of the process that will reduce any negative impacts without compromising the bottom line or anticipated systemic outcome. It is an integrated, holistic approach that promotes compromise and tradeoffs.

Figure 1.0 presents the copyrighted schematic for ED4SP©. In parts two, three, and four, we will discuss ED4SP© as applicable to an individual, an organization or organizational cluster, and jurisdiction or jurisdictional cluster.

Figure 1.0 Copyrighted Schematic for ED4SP©

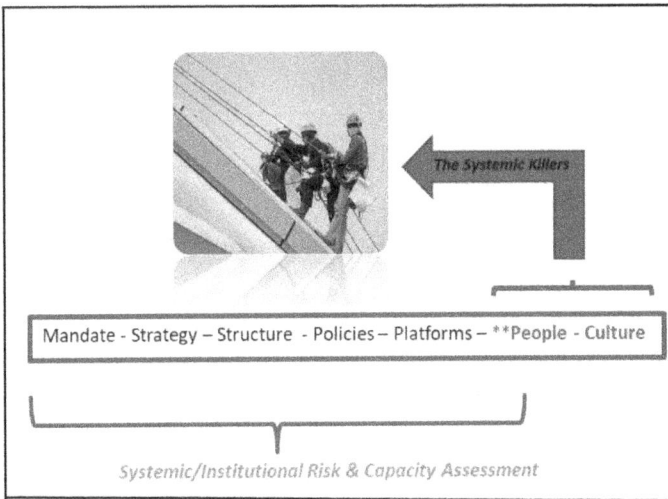

© Newman, L.S (2021)

The Oxford dictionary defines an 'entity' as *"a thing with distinct and independent existence"*. One can, as such, infer that an entity can exist in different formats and arrangements, but even if entities exist in different formats and arrangements, they could have similar base frameworks and features that are similar to most. The ED4SP© recognizes this reality and, within systems-thinking, explains how an 'entity', be it an individual, an organization, or a jurisdiction, can attain sustainable performance through various life cycle stages of the 'entity'. The components of the ED4SP© concept and the relationship between the components are basic requirements that need to be defined and aligned harmoniously with the following eight aspects of an 'entity':

The Mandate: This is what the entity seeks to achieve,

41

what it represents and whom it is set to serve.

The Strategy: This is how the entity plans to go about attaining its mandate and to what end.

The Structure: Describes how the entity arranges the various roles within the entity in pursuit of the Mandate and Strategy. It also identifies the relationships that exist between the various bodies that make up the whole.

Policies: This considers the various provisions within which the entity will operate. It identifies the processes required to attain the defined objectives; what rules exist to guide how these processes are carried out at various levels within the structure as defined.

Platforms: This relates to the levels of engagement for application, storage, retrieval, dissemination, and disclosures to stakeholders within and externally.

People: This identifies the type of people required to work within the entity's various roles as defined in the structure. How will they be selected, placed, monitored, and eliminated or rewarded?

Culture: This is the social contract that exists within the entity on how the entity engages people at various levels and how should those whom the entity serves expect to be served.

Systemic or Institutional Risk and Capacity Assessment: What are the issues that can compromise the attainment of the entity's mandate? How can they be identified, measured, and nipped in the bud?

In Parts Two, Three, and Four of *African Leaders' Tête À Tête*, we will see how these eight components of the ED4SP© differ and transition in situations applicable to an individual, an organization or an organizational cluster as well as a jurisdiction or jurisdictional cluster using pseudo samples. After reviewing the pseudo ED4SP© samples for individual, organizational, and jurisdictional situations, you will have space in the book to jot down your thoughts as you sketch your own scenarios from our discussion, either in hard copy or digital format, depending on your preferred copy.

3

SWOTPlus©

Lacy, Long & Spindler (2020), in their book, <u>The Circular Economy Handbook: Realizing The Circular Advantage</u>, said, *"Complex and interconnected challenges are changing the face of how [entities] need to think, work and innovate. Rising political and geo-economic tensions, the pace and scale of technological change, along with the urgency of climate crises, resource scarcity, and a myriad of other social and environmental issues are dramatically altering the landscape".*

SWOTPlus© is an acronym that I created to extend the application of the popular strategic planning tool, SWOT (Strength, Weaknesses, Opportunities, and Threat), by including entity implementation with suggested resource allocation and timelines. In arriving at this concept, I leveraged various situations over the course of my career, where I have had the privilege of participating in my employers' strategic planning, supporting a client organization with their own strategic planning, or handholding advisory support to boards. Over the years, I have particularly found SWOT to be a very useful tool. However, as I gained more experience and got involved in deeper aspects of strategic planning, which involved resourcing the strategy plan and monitoring implementation over the plan period, I started to observe some limitations of carrying the SWOT analysis through, which felt like standing on the edge of a cliff. In that situation, while applying problem-solving skills to walk myself beyond the limitations, I developed and started to use a two-by-two matrix as a personal extension of SWOT.

As a student of SWOT, I later read Gurel's (2017) theoretical review of SWOT as a planning tool. I was intrigued by this critical analysis because it explained the position of SWOT Analysis in the strategic management process. The study reported that components of SWOT Analysis were examined, showing the historical origins of SWOT, advantages-disadvantages, and the limitations of SWOT. The study concluded that "SWOT Analysis has been used over the last fifty years in the field of strategic management, and it is a valuable technique for planning and decision making. Over the years, SWOT has been a widely used technique in analysing internal and external environments to support strategic decision situations. The technique has been employed in myriad areas demanding strategic analysis for an industry, an organization, a product, a person, a project, a city, etc. Despite being a simple managerial tool with many advantages in the planning process, disadvantages and limitations also abound. For instance, the study reported that *"SWOT Analysis presents a mere list of factors as to micro and macro environment. It is difficult to use qualitatively listed factors in decision-making. The qualitative examination of the internal and external factors can only be a beginning for an in-depth analysis in the planning process".* I got so excited about this study, so much so that it became my business case for the implementation challenges I was having, which led me to develop the two-by-two matrix, now copyrighted as SWOTPlus©, honouring the past but extending into the new.

Figure 2.0 presents the schematic for SWOTPlus©. In parts two, three, and four of this body of work, we will discuss SWOTPlus© as applicable to an individual, an organization or organizational cluster, and jurisdiction or jurisdictional cluster.

Figure 2.0 Copyrighted Schematic for SWOTPlus©

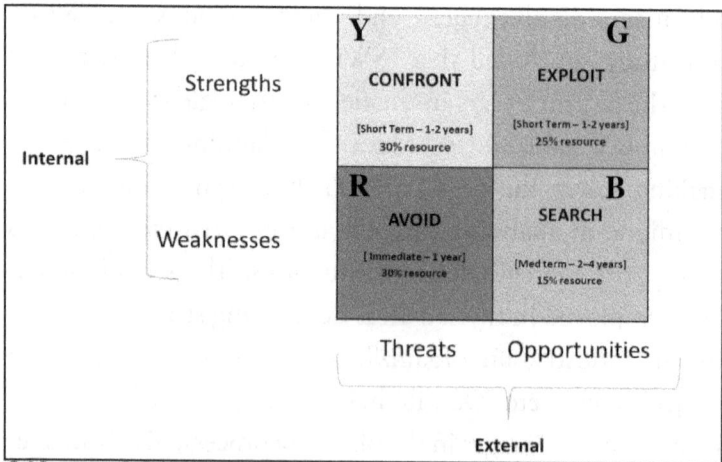

© Newman, L.S (2021)

Explanation Of *Figure 2.0*

Strengths and weaknesses are internal and relatively controllable via objective structure, policies, processes, roles, people, and resource allocation, as well as control and compliance. On the other hand, opportunities and threats are external and are relatively uncontrollable, but the capacity to thrive and stay at the edge is enhanced with effective and practical market intelligence, alliance building, networking, and speed to market, based on validated facts.

The Four Quadrants

- **R** – What is both an internal weakness to the entity and an external threat to the entity or entity system? This is a killer and must be addressed urgently to move to the Y or B zone.

- **B** – What is an internal weakness to the entity but has potential external opportunities to entity or entity type or system? This is an area to invest in, learn more about, and plan a strategy to enhance internal strength and move to the Y zone.

- **Y** – What is an internal strength to the entity but a threat externally to the entity or entity system? This is a good one to be conquered and converted to a G zone for harvest.

- **G** – What is an internal strength to the entity and has opportunities externally for the entity and entity type or system? These are low-hanging fruits that should be harvested urgently because, depending on industry dynamism, the situation may not last!

Part One Takeaways

Part one of the *African Leaders' Tête À Tête*, aptly titled, "The Lion's Gaze", contained three chapters and extended the issues discussed in "Introduction" by setting the context of the key discussion themes within the book, being an Africa-focused conversation, using two schematic concepts on entity design and prioritization for systemic outcomes, referred to as "ED4SP©" and "SWOTPlus©"

In setting the focus within the context of Africa, chapter one provided information on Africa's physical location, historical context, current state, foreseeable future and areas of concern for further consideration, thus, technically providing the business case for the themes for the book.

In Chapter Two, I explained ED4SP© within the contextual body of knowledge, while in chapter three, I did the same for SWOTPlus©. Both ED4SP© and SWOTPlus© were copyrighted in 2021 and are the tools that I will be using in situations applicable to the individual, organization or organizational clusters, jurisdiction or jurisdictional clusters in parts two, three, and four of *African Leaders' Tête À Tête*. In Part Two, you and I will apply ED4SP© and SWOTPlus© to the individual situation, using a pseudo personality, Human X, as a sample to guide you in deriving your own personal journey of positioning for constructive contribution to Africa as an emerging market.

PART TWO
The Individual

"Leadership is ultimately about creating a way for people to contribute to making something extraordinary happen." – **Alan Keith.**

Have you ever belonged to or been part of a group where an individual took control of the situation by conveying a comprehensible vision of the group's goals, a distinct passion for the work, and an ability to make everyone in the group feel recharged and energized, inspiring positive changes in them? This not only sounds like an individual who is an effective leader but a transformational leader. The resultant effect of transformational leadership is a group of engaged and productive people who are empowered to innovate and help shape an organization, community, or nation's future success.

From the Hawthorne experiments of the 1920s about illumination and production levels to the extended Elton Mayo germinal management theory about the social aspect of industrial psychology as a factor of productivity, humanity has, in the quest for attaining more with less, continued to focus on various aspects of what and how of arranging human endeavours for systemic outcomes, with many more germinal leadership theories on influence and impact, right up to the modern day concepts such as the transformational leadership concept. The subject of leadership is complex, elaborate, and increasingly attracting interest at the individual, corporate, national, and global levels because times and events are changing very fast!

The world as we know it is becoming more integrated and dynamic, political boundaries are becoming increasingly illusive, society is becoming more knowledgeable about rights and privileges, and the physical and conceptual environment for enterprise, life and living is becoming more turbulent, aided by the role of technology, speed of information and shared platforms. Africa, Africans, and friends or residents of Africa are in this mix. Africa is in transformation! The Big question is, how can we position ourselves to contribute to this trajectory for systemic outcomes and legacy? Positioning for success in this trajectory has everything to do with leadership, precisely, transformational leadership. Such is the leadership that transforms potential into reality. I believe leadership-related issues in Africa are varied, including resource management and investments, addressing poverty, social responsibility, accountability and good governance. We all want to chip in!

Back in the day, based on findings as a product development manager with a Nigerian bank, I recall that many Nigerians in the diaspora wanted to own property back home to serve as country homes when they visit with their families. As a result, many diasporans requested the support of family members back home and friends, in some cases, to oversee the construction of such homes on their behalf. However, many tales of woe emanated from these "projects". So, my employer then – the bank, developed a banking product that enabled the diaspora families to buy or build their homes back home, with the bank providing payment and product supervision services for a fee. It was a very successful product because it had a ready market, and the bank had access to many diaspora people then. I had the privilege of being on the product development and management team for this particular product and others under the leadership of a dynamic leadership team. In view of this experience and many others, I can appreciate the challenges of our diaspora brothers and sisters looking into Africa to participate in the opportunities as individuals and families.

In getting us started, I would like to start by walking us through the ED4SP© concept as applicable to us as individuals, and then, based on a sample ED4SP© applicable to a depersonalized individual "entity", you may develop your own ED4SP©. Thereafter, we will also review the SWOTPlus© for our depersonalized individual entity Human X so that you can develop yours. If we do this right, you should be able to clearly see what is most important to you as a leader looking in on Africa or looking out to the world from within Africa for positive systemic outcomes.

Figure 3.0 is the schematic that we will use for individual ED4SP©, and Figure 4.0 is the schematic that we will use for individual SWOTPlus©. This process promises to be fun! So, like Fareed Zakaria of the CNN programme, the Global Public Square (GPS) would say at the commencement of each episode, "let's get started!"

53

Psuedo Personality Human X Profile

Our pseudo personality in Part Two will be Human X, a 45-year-old person that is of African extraction from Uganda, now living in Los Angeles. Human X is a parent of three young adults between the ages of 19 and 25. Human X was formerly an employee of a Fortune 500 company with Administration, Human Resources, and Information Technology experiences but now runs a small business, operating from home in Los Angeles, as a freelance person. Also, Human X is an active member of the Uganda Diaspora Community in the United States and other related professional networks. We will use Human X's ED4SP© and SWOTPlus© to guide our discussion of the two concepts as applicable to the individual leader.

4

The Concepts

Concepts here refer to the leadership concepts for the individual leader. Whether taking on a leadership role for a complex project or advancing in your life goals, leadership concepts are practical tools you can use to develop your strengths in your endeavours. Thus, leadership concepts refer to factors that individual leaders consider when applying themselves and overseeing a project or team of individuals. Simply put, leadership concepts encompass the styles, traits, and principles of different approaches to managing a project or a team on a project. These concepts help individuals understand what they require to make meaningful progress in their careers and impact society.

Now that we have established the importance of these concepts for the individual leader, let's try to understand it better with some essential concepts using our pseudo personality, Human X, as a sample.

ED4SP© Narration With Human X In View As A Sample

Figure 3.0 Schematic for Human X ED4SP©

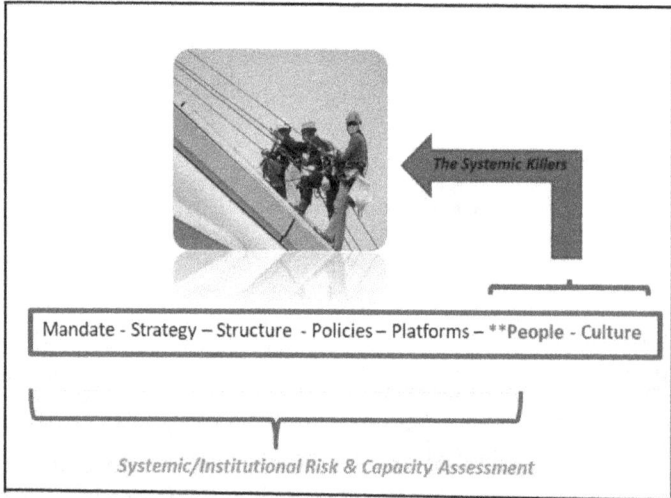

© Newman, L.S (2021)

The Mandate: Defining your mandate as a person requires that you think about your aspired contribution to humanity in general, then your community, country, and Africa. In defining this, you will need to define what you want to attain in your life's journey, leveraging your past and future legacy within the next ten years in Africa's journey. One's faith or belief system, as well as a personal mantra, can be helpful in scoping this. Then, narrow this to whom your defined mandate will serve. Rosenberg's (2020) five sectors described towards the end of Chapter 1 in Part One may be helpful. You will need to decide where and how you would like to participate. Is it in the private, public, or nonprofit sector? Also, which sector cluster? Is it the extractive, processing and manufacturing or services, innovation and knowledge, or policy and social services? Then, which geographical location in Africa?

Sample For Human X:

I am a 45-year-old African from Uganda living in Los Angeles. As a former employee of a Fortune 500 company in the US, now a small business owner with young adult children, and given my field as a professional, I appreciate the African youth demographics and the risks it portends, if not well harnessed. As such, I would like to positively impact Ugandan youth employability and their acquisition of modern work and entrepreneurial skills, starting with my community and then, maybe after the first two years, my municipality, then in the third phase, my province, and the country as a whole after a decade, if I gain traction and support.

The Strategy: Here, you will need to define how you plan to go about attaining your mandate as defined and to what end. Do you want to attain it as a private individual, a network, a family project, a foundation, or a voluntary service?

Sample For Human X:

I would like to support young Ugandans learn 21st-century employability and entrepreneurial skills so that they can be employable, and those who want to run businesses can do so effectively and successfully. I will be participating in the nonprofit arena in the fourth sector, which is Innovation and Knowledge. I will also explore ways of supporting the Ugandan government with policies that can positively impact youth development remotely and visit pro bono via the Ugandan diaspora community in the US. I will plan for the first two years and then review at the end of the second year for a three-year plan. I will review things at the end of my fourth year to plan for the next five years. Hopefully, I would see a systemic impact by the end of a decade of such support.

The Structure: Describes how you plan to arrange your various roles as an individual in pursuit of the mandate and strategy already described above. You will also need to identify the stakeholder relationships within your various roles that constitute "YOU". That is within your nuclear and extended family in terms of your inner circle members, professional network, diaspora network, and social network. Doing this will help you notice relationships that you would have otherwise missed out on or not optimized.

Sample For Human X:

I will leverage my professional and social networks for businesses with corporate social responsibility interests in supporting Africa to partner so that I can serve as a volunteer on projects linked to my defined mandate. I will also try and make personal visits to applicable ministries on my next trip to Kampala, with a referral from the Ugandan

Embassy in Washington DC.

Policies: Here, you will need to consider the various provisions within which you will operate. That is your own principles and values, personal philosophies and belief systems, family social contract, professional code of ethics, workplace standards for personal conduct, legal provisions of your place of residence, like state laws, constitution, etc. If you are a diaspora African, you will also need to work within the constitutional provisions of your home country in Africa. These 'policies' will help you identify the processes you will require to legitimately attain your defined strategic objectives with a sense of personal fulfilment, and also what rules exist to guide how these aspirations and processes are carried out at various levels of your personal life. Tax laws, residency principles, banking provisions, and residency or indigene provisions have limitations and privileges. You will need to establish the boundaries within which you can pursue your aspirations for your space of endeavour in the country and continent you choose.

Sample For Human X:

I will study the constitutional and company law provisions for international development related to Corporate Social Responsibility (CSR) in the innovation and knowledge sector cluster, as applicable to youth for US corporates, in order to find alignments with the Sustainable Development Goals (SDGs) and Agenda 2063 in Uganda's National

Plan. I will also study the US tax laws and opportunities for short exchange programs or virtual seminars to and from Africa. In view of emerging opportunities in Africa, I would like my children to connect with their roots; as such, I will encourage their participation in exchange programs with NGOs working in this area as well as their participation in my seminars for Uganda youths.

Platforms: Here, you will need to review the roles you defined in the structure, and within the limitations and provisions of the "policies", determine the levels of engagement for application, storage, retrieval, dissemination, and disclosures to stakeholders internally and externally. How will you engage? – Family meetings, social media, visits to your country, attendance of diaspora events, visibility in your professional networks, or advisory services to the Ugandan government? The platforms you choose will need to be either already existing or emerging in the spaces you defined under "Mandate". If the platforms don't exist, you will need to decide to either build such a platform from scratch or buy.

Sample For Human X:
I will start with free online workshops targeted at Ugandan youths, which I will publicize via my social media handle, the Ugandan Embassy in the US, the Ugandan diaspora network, and corporates with interest in African youth development and exchange programs to see what opportunities exist and how I can start and then scale up. I

will also research and get the email and telephone contact details of all registered schools in Uganda catering to students ages 13 to 25.

People: This consideration is technically about making enrolment decisions. You will need to identify the type of people required to work with you in your various roles as defined under "Structure". How will they be selected, placed, elevated from outer circle to inner circle and moved around roles, monitored, and eliminated or rewarded along the journey as defined by your mandate and the "Platforms" of engagement? Having this clear in your mind and documented for your private use will help you deal with future successes, failures, conflicts, need for separation and replacements as you keep your lion's gaze on your "Mandate". Many individuals have experienced mandate derailments and disappointments due to not paying attention to this aspect.

Sample For Human X:

I will send information about the online workshops to the applicable ministries in Uganda under the Ugandan diaspora networks. Schools within the specified age group will also be contacted to allow cross-locational capacity impact in all regions across Uganda, just in case, starting with a quarterly process that can be assessed and made monthly in the second year. In the first year, I will look out for partners and schools that would like to adapt the free seminars and workshops as part of their off-syllabus curriculum. The only requirement by partner schools will be a hall where students can gather and participate, access to electricity and internet, and a projector, which they should provide since the content and resource person will be free.

Culture: This is the social contract you should have with your "People" on how you interact at various levels and how those you wish to serve, as defined in the "Mandate", expect to be served. Clearly defining this will help enhance the efficiency of your interventions, save you money, and provide the synergy to scale up for systemic impact. The reverse can be the case if this is not well defined, communicated to all parties and understood. Many leaders have experienced failed projects as a result of this aspect of entity design not being well thought through.

Sample For Human X:
Partner schools and workshop locations will be required to take attendance and remit names, gender, telephone, and email contact of all participants at all sessions, to enable my team in Los Angeles to track the numbers, send workshop materials to participants, and provide one-on-one post-session coaching to the participants. As I see the commitment from the schools and community centres, I will make plans to underwrite their costs on internet access and electricity. When I see the commitment from the partner school and community centres over the first year, I will ship projectors as a reward for performance to part-ner schools, based on attendance numbers and outcomes

of the workshops on the graduating sets. However, partner schools that fail to meet this requirement over two workshop periods will be placed on probation and only be readmitted after submitting the required information for the full period of support. Local coordinators and administrators at partner schools will also, over a period of six months and based on their performance in terms of timeliness of reports submitted, be upgraded to benefit from three monthly one-on-one coaching sessions with me as an incentive to keep doing well.

Systemic or Institutional Risk and Capacity

Assessment: For you to adequately undertake this, you will need to mentally detach yourself from the plans, review past failures of others for patterns and correlation, and then possibly ask your significant other to specifically look over everything with you to find "what can go wrong" with your own aspired project. What are the issues that can compromise the attainment of your mandate? How can they be identified, measured, and nipped in the bud? Do you need an insurance policy, further study, or specialist oversight by another entity at ground level zero under a formal contract? Will you consider a partnership with an entity that has the infrastructure on the ground to run the project on your behalf? Do you have the administrative capacity, time, or access to supervise the implementation of your 'mandate'? What will it cost you in terms of time and resources for the first two years and the next three years, as you indicated? How will you meet this resource need?

Sample For Human X:

Likely issues that can compromise this intervention include:

(a) My ability to commit to the number and days for the work.

(b) My adequate preparation for the workshops with materials that resonate with the participants.

(c) An assistant to help me with record keeping, analysis, reporting and tracking of participants, and scheduling of coaching sessions.

(d) Access to school authorities and the ministry of youth development in Uganda via the Ugandan Embassy in the US.

(e) In case of any health challenges or misfortunes, what will happen to this plan, and how do I ensure continuity if I am not available?

(f) I will need to be open to collaborating with other Ugandans in the diaspora and in Uganda on this initiative.

On the part of the partner schools:
(1) Continuity of the seminars beyond leadership change situations.

(2) Access to electricity.

(3) Applicable approvals from supervising ministries and regulatory agencies.

(4) Possibility of sabotage from contending individuals that

can compromise the attainment of my mandate.

I will need to ensure that I identify the early signals and take steps to ensure these factors do not contend with my "Mandate" and "Strategy". For this reason, I will plan for the first two years, after which I will review and plan for the next five years, all being well.

SWOTPlus© Narration With Human X In View As A Sample

Figure 4.0 Schematic for Human X SWOTPlus©

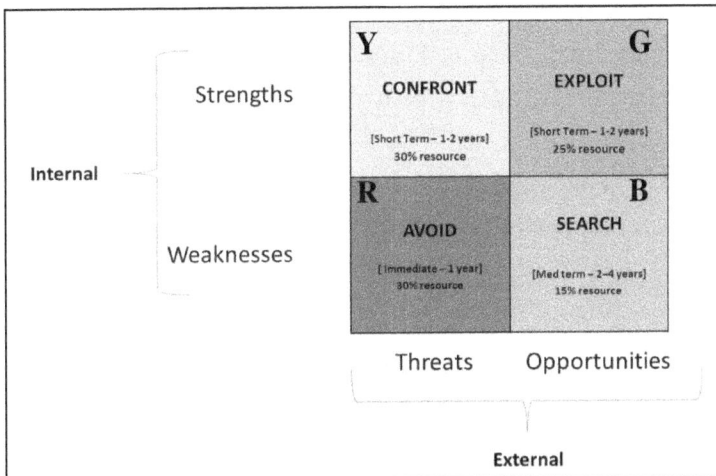

© Newman, L.S (2021)

Application of *Figure 4.0* to Human X

Human X's strengths and weaknesses are internal and

relatively controllable by Human X from personal choices and decisions. On the other hand, opportunities and threats are external to Human X and relatively uncontrollable. However, Human X's capacity to thrive and stay ahead of challenges is enhanced with effective intelligence gathering, constructive engagements, negotiations, alliance building, leveraging applicable networks based on validated facts and being open to new ideas.

Likely Contents of the Four Quadrants for Human X:

- **R** – What is both an internal weakness to Human X and an external threat to Human X? This is a dream killer! It must be addressed urgently to move to the Y or B zone.

- **B** – What is an internal weakness to Human X but has potential external opportunities to Human X? This is an area to invest in, find out more, and plan strategy to enhance internal strength and move to Y zone.

- **Y** – What is an internal strength to Human X but a threat externally to Human X? This is a good one to be conquered and converted to a G zone for harvest.

- **G** – What is an internal strength to Human X and has opportunities externally for Human X? These are low-hanging fruits that should be harvested urgently because, depending on industry dynamism, the situation may not last!

Figure 5.0 Human X SWOTPlus© for the first two years.

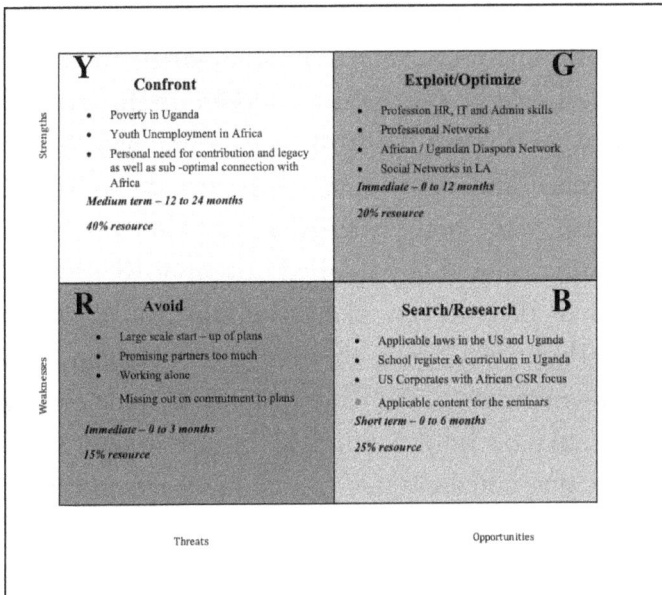

Y Confront	**Exploit/Optimize** **G**
Strengths • Poverty in Uganda • Youth Unemployment in Africa • Personal need for contribution and legacy as well as sub-optimal connection with Africa *Medium term – 12 to 24 months* *40% resource*	• Profession HR, IT and Admin skills • Professional Networks • African / Ugandan Diaspora Network • Social Networks in LA *Immediate – 0 to 12 months* *20% resource*
R Avoid	Search/Research **B**
Weaknesses • Large scale start – up of plans • Promising partners too much • Working alone • Missing out on commitment to plans *Immediate – 0 to 3 months* *15% resource*	• Applicable laws in the US and Uganda • School register & curriculum in Uganda • US Corporates with African CSR focus • Applicable content for the seminars *Short term – 0 to 6 months* *25% resource*
Threats	Opportunities

Narration of *Figure 5.0* Human X SWOTPlus© For the First Two Years

Human X is able to derive the applicable SWOTPlus© because the ED4SP© was well aligned. Therefore,

1. Contents of the four quadrants for Human X were very clear in terms of strategic focus for what to avoid, search further, confront, and exploit.

2. Clarity of entity design in descriptive terms also helped list the key issues in each quadrant.

3. In view of this clarity and Human X's plan for three-time blocks of two years, three years, and five years, it is easy to set priorities for the first two years. What to avoid, which are both personal weaknesses to Human x and external threats to the program, should be addressed within zero to three months. Areas of opportunities but weaknesses to Human X should be researched and ascertained within zero to six months. Areas that are both strengths to Human X and opportunities should be exploited or optimized within the first year of the two-year plan or within half of the plan period. Then lastly, areas of strength to Human X but external weaknesses in the target "Mandate" and "Strategy" space should be fully confronted in the second year to have systemic outcomes that can be measured and help in planning the next three years' time block. Repeat the same after the second plan period.

4. Leveraging on (4) above, Human X is able to get resources to each strategic focus area. This process will help Human X manage the initiative's cash, time, and material commitment. The percentage of resources allocated for the plan period take-off should always add up to 100 percent.

5. With this arrangement, Human X will be able to see the systemic outcome of the intervention in Uganda and scale up or adjust on a time-block basis.

6. The overall objective is also to ensure that issues are

addressed, and they likely get moved to other areas. For example, when addressed, items in the R zone should move to the Y or B zone. In the next plan period, items in the B zone can be in the G zone if converted to strength and still an opportunity. When confronted, items in the Y zone naturally move to the G zone.

7. Human X will ensure that nothing moves from the Y, B, or G zone into the R zone by staying informed and watchful to know when to shift the project focus. That is what the milestones in the second and fifth years will help attain.

Summary of Individual ED4SP© and SWOTPlus©

In Chapter Four, we saw how ED4SP© and SWOTPlus© could apply to an individual using a pseudo personality, Human X. We also saw how paying close attention to ED4SP© helps the process of applying SWOTPlus©. Thus, affirming that the two concepts go together and ED4SP© should ALWAYS be addressed before SWOTPlus© for optimal outcomes. Now it is your turn to leverage our discussions from the Author's Note to the Introduction and Chapters One to Four and derive your personal ED4SP© and SWOTPlus© for your initial plan period. I am excited and look forward to Chapter Five and your feedback after completion.

5

Reflections On
The Concepts

According to Swart, Price, Mann, and Brown (2004), given increasing awareness that "ideas for innovation, quality, and continuous improvement, [including] other critically important inputs needed to compete in the modern, highly competitive business world of today come from people". Emerging observations about Africa as triggered by the Sustainable Development Goals (SDGs) and Agenda 2063 indicate that Africa appears to be on the edge of a major landscape shift, and the outcome of that shift will be dependent on one key factor – leadership practices at various levels within Africa looking outward and by Africans in the diaspora looking inward to Africa.

In this perspective, Hayatu-Deen (2002) predicted that: *"Organizations and countries who understand the new world economy and who grasp [emerging] interdependent and interconnected nature, who master the art of positioning themselves to take advantage of opportunities and deal with the threats posed by such a world can lay claim to prosperity and greatness".*

Also, Charan (2009), in the book, <u>Leadership In The Era of Economic Uncertainty: New Rule for Getting The Right Things Done In Difficult Times</u>, listed six essential leadership traits for hard times as follows:
(1) Honesty and credibility.
(2) The ability to inspire.
(3) Realism tempered with optimism.
(4) Real-time connection with reality.
(5) Managing with intensity.
(6) Boldness in building for the future.

Definitely, this is our time! Discussions like this need to help us collaboratively discuss how we can contribute to this promising future for Africa with profoundly gratifying and high-impact systemic outcomes. The big question is – given what we have so far discussed, your experience, social and professional networks, love for Africa, and resources at your disposal, how would you like to participate?

To start, I kindly request that you define yourself by answering the questions below:
i. Your Name, Age, Situation?

ii. Where do you live? – Country, State, County, City.

iii. What experience and skills do you have?

iv. What part of Africa are you from, or what part of Africa would you like to support? What are the challenges in that area in Africa?

v. Which of your skills can you readily convert to help? Which sector would you like to help? Which of your social and professional networks can support this aspiration?

vi. How do you want to support? Is it by being on ground in Africa or working in partnership with entities on ground in Africa?

ED4SP© Narration for *(Your name)*

• Your Personality Profile (*Obtainable from responses to i - vi*)

- Your Mandate *(Based on the profile)*

- Your Strategy *(Approach to attaining the Mandate)*

- Structure *(Roles required to attain your Mandate and Strategy)*

- Policies *(The legal boundaries to your Mandate)*

- Platforms *(For stakeholder engagement on Mandate and Strategy)*

- People *(People you need, how to enroll, train, and assess them)*

- Culture *(Your social culture with stakeholders and supporters)*

- Systemic Risk and Capacity Assessment *(Managing the red flags)*

I have a few questions that I would like us to reflect on before extending the ED4SP© you just developed:

- How did you feel about the process?

- Have you had other personal projects in Africa?

- How did the projects go?

- Were there challenges in attaining the strategic objectives of those projects?

- Knowing what you know now with the ED4SP© concept, would you have done something differently? If yes, what would you have done differently?

- How would applying the ED4SP© concept to these

projects have impacted your former projects?

We will now proceed to guide you in extending the various components of your personal ED4SP© into your personal SWOTPlus©, as applicable to your defined ED4SP©. I hope you have as much fun doing this as I would like to believe you did in drafting your personal ED4SP©.

SWOTPlus© Narration For *(Your name)*

*Figure 6.0 SWOTPlus© for (Your name)*_____
*for (Number of years)*_____
(Best to plan for two to three years at the first instance).

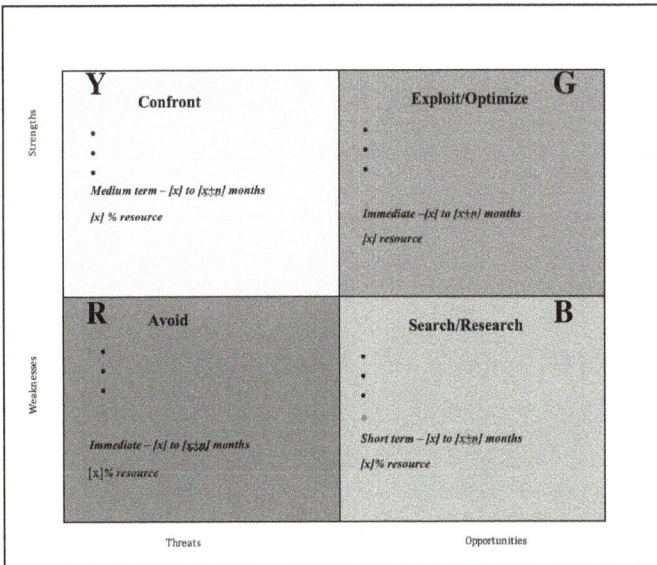

© Newman, L.S (2021)

You will need to visit *figure 5.0* and its narrations to now narrate yours. Bullet points 1 to 8 on the narrations will need to apply to yours in *figure 6.0* above:

1. ....
....
....
....
....

2. ....
....
....
....
....

3. ....
....
....
....
....

4. ....
....
....
....
....

5. ....

....
....
....
....

6. ....
....
....
....
....

7. ....
....
....
....
....

8. ....
....
....
....
....

Part Two Takeaways

Part Two, aptly titled *"The Individual"*, contained two chapters which addressed a review of the two concepts ED4SP© and SWOTPlus©, as well as a reflection on the concepts based on which you developed your own ED4SP© and SWOTPlus© using your observations from the pseudo–Human X process. I have enjoyed this process and hope the process will be useful to your personal journey of contributing to Africa's transformation in your personal capacity.

In Part Three, you and I will apply ED4SP© and SWOTPlus© to an organizational situation, using a pseudo sample, Organization Y, to guide you in deriving your choice organization for an apt positioning as a participant in Africa's journey to Agenda 2063: *The Africa We Want.*

PART THREE
Organizations

"Organizations are diverse and complex but have some basic elements that are similar to most organizations, and these include the organization's social structure, participants, or social actors, goals, technology, and environment." – **William Richard Scott** (2003).

In a similar perspective as the above statement, Gupta and Govindarajan (2004) explained that as we witness growing economic interdependence among countries, several levels of aggregation of the organization would tend to result in the following areas:

• Market presence.

• Supply chain.

• Capital base.

• Corporate mindset or human capital.

In view of this, corporate arrangements need to be well thought through because operating environments are getting more dynamic and increasingly integrated due to developments linked to globalization, technology, and mobility of humanity with fluid boundaries that hitherto served as restraints to mobility. For more clarity, one of my mentors and friend at the International Society for Performance Improvement, Addison (2004), in his article on corporate architecture, said, *"Performance architecture is the design of the organizational house where all three levels are integrated to smoothly support the raison d'etre of the entity, be it a business, civil service, or non-governmental organization"*. Addison's timeless proposition relates to organizational design to facilitate performance management and some aspects of benchmarking, including:

(a) Establishing appropriate goals.

(b) Monitoring performance through internal and external feedback.

(c) Taking corrective action if needed.

(d) Communicating appropriately.

(e) Allocating resources to support the efficient achievement of goals.

(f) Making sure that all parts of the organization cooperate effectively to achieve the organization's purpose.

ED4SP© and SWOTPlus© attempt to show how to achieve all these and more on a simplistic and sustainable basis.

With the African Continental Free Trade Agreement (AfCFTA), we noted in Chapter One that Africa is now home to the world's largest free trade area and a fast-growing, almost 1.4-billion-person market. A close observation of the United Nations' Sustainable Development Goals [SDGs], also known as Agenda 2030, shows seven key aspirations of the programme, with 37 priority areas. As described in Chapter One, the African Union's half-a-century strategic transformation plan, Agenda 2063, also tends to align with SDG broad themes. All of these seem to naturally find expression in key objectives of the

83

AfCTFA as a catalyst for opening Africa to Africa and to the world.

As leaders, most of us want to leave legacies in systems that we have had the opportunity to lead. Because of this, many corporate leaders fail to realize from day one that there is a day to leave that leadership role. Long before I got into my former role as CEO, I found one of the late distinguished Colin Powell's quotes most helpful as it inspired me to set a digital 60-month countdown on my computer from the first day of each of my two five-year terms in office. Each day I logged in during the first five years, it told me how much more time I had in office in months, days, hours, minutes, and seconds. After my tenure was extended and I got a second five-year term, I continued the same process. However, one of the first things I did during my second term in office was to serve my notice about a plan to take early retirement at the end of the second term for career transition into a new space. The Colin Powel quote that kept me on my toes and helped me reinvent my leadership space at most of my career milestones states: *"Avoid having your ego so close to your position that when your position falls, your ego goes with it"*. As a result of many factors, including this quote, the roles I occupy have never defined me. So, with your consent, let us note this quote as you seek ways to make contributions via your organization as a leader.

Additionally, on a more cheerful note and in view of your

decision to discuss this section with me, I would like to share something else I found useful in my former role as a CEO and consultant to corporates operating in Africa facing outward. I have documented this insight in Newman (2020) – *Storytelling: An African Leadership Journey of Performance Improvement Innovation*, a book chapter in Van Tiem and Burns (2020), <u>Cases On Performance Improvement Innovation</u>, published by IGI Global; my contribution to this publication was the only submission about Africa. In the chapter, I alluded to having found Kaufman's (2006) listing of three basic essentials of achieving sustained success very helpful. The three essentials were listed as follows:

(1) A societal value-added frame of mind.

(2) A shared determination and agreement on where to head and why.

(3) Use consistent application of pragmatic and basic tools.

I continue to treasure the opportunity of meeting and severally interacting with the distinguished late Roger Kaufman at several ISPI conferences and events in the US from 2001 to 2019 before he passed on in 2020. With this mindset, I leveraged my former organization's Platform and Mandate as a not-for-profit limited by guarantee organizations with membership consisting of regulators and operators in Nigeria's banking industry to put the ten Kaufman questions for Mega Planning and Thinking into actual scenarios severally in that role. The organization mainly provided professional services to Nigeria's financial services, but its clientele cut across all sectors, including international subsidiaries of members and regional professional networks in Africa. Overall, the referenced had a platform of over 1570 stakeholder organizations within the Nigerian Financial Services Sector and beyond. So, my colleagues in management and the board had two five-year planning cycles. Together, we deployed many interventions as an entity and also supported many of our clients navigate their own paths. In this role, I particularly found the ten Kaufman questions for Mega Planning useful for personal reflection at each key milestone in my career.

As we proceed to develop the ED4SP© and SWOTPlus© applicable to an organization and organizational clusters, I kindly request that you first revisit Rosenberg's (2020) nomenclatures of sectors as discussed in Chapter One to identify your current or target organization or cluster or organization[s]' sector as Private, Public, or Non-Profit sector, based on ownership. Thereafter, confirm the sector cluster categorization as primary [extractive], or secondary [processing or manufacturing], or tertiary [services], or quaternary [innovations and knowledge], or quintenary [policy making at national, sub-national, and social sector]. If you are playing a leadership role in a group structure or conglomerate or overseeing a ministry or industry regulator, many of these sector clusters may be applicable to your organization entity. Secondly, try to dispassionately answer the following ten Kaufman Mega Planning questions to derive a profile for your organization or cluster of organizations. The questions are:

Q1 - Do you care about your success and legacy as a leader?

Q2 - Do you care about societal well-being and value-added?

Q3 - Do you care about your organization's success?

Q4 - Do you care about the usefulness of what your organization delivers to its clients and society at large within Africa or to Africa?

Q5 - Do you care about the quality of what you deliver to your clients?

Q6 - Do you care about the quality of products from your organization[s]?

Q7 - Do you care about your organization's operational efficiency and compliance?

Q8 - Do you care about the availability and quality of resources?

Q9 - Do you care whether your organization meets its strategic objectives?

Q10 - Are you concerned about the value of what you do and how you do things?

Another big question is – how can we position your organization to contribute to its chosen space for systemic outcomes and sustained impact?

I would like to start by walking through the ED4SP© concept as applicable to a pseudo–Organization Y and then, based on this sample, guide you to develop your choice organization's ED4SP©. Thereafter, we will also review the SWOTPlus© for our pseudo–Organization Y so that you can develop yours. If we do this right, you should be able to clearly see what is most important to your organizational context in Africa's trajectory. *Figure 7.0* is the Organization Y schematic that we will use for ED4SP©, and *Figure 8.0* is Organization Y SWOTPlus©. To get started, we need to profile our sample organization as we did for our pseudo personality, Human X.

Psuedo Organization Y Profile

Our pseudo-organization in Part Three is Organization Y, a 120 years old conglomerate with headquarters in Addis Ababa, Ethiopia and subsidiaries in Egypt, South Africa, Senegal, the Dominican Republic of Congo [DRC], and Tanzania. The group is a private sector operator listed on the Addis Ababa stock exchange. It operates across three of the five Rosenberg's [2020] sector clusters, namely:

(a) The primary sector because of its farms in Egypt, the DRC, and Senegal.

(b) The secondary cluster, because of its processing plants with light manufacturing for exports, in Egypt, Senegal, and the DRC.

(c) Within the tertiary sector, because of its logistics services and wholesale merchandising outlets in all its six locations across Africa.

Organization Y has been a strong advocate of the 17 Global Goals, also known as the Sustainable Development Goals (SDGs). The 17 SDGs are enshrined in Organization Y's group governance codes applicable to raw materials sourcing, employment, service resourcing, operational administration, and corporate social responsibility engagements with its host communities and governments. Organization Y is now studying the implications of the AfCFTA to its operations and relationship with suppliers and service providers, being a proudly African modern enterprise.

In view of this profile, Organization Y wants to positively impact Africa's journey to Agenda 2063: *The Africa We Want.* Consequently, the group has drawn on various partnerships across continents to build capacity for systemic outcomes. For purposes of our discussion, we will focus on the group as a whole. In real life, to ensure wholesome coverage, the group ED4SP© and SWOTPlus© should be cascaded down to have an ED4SP© and a SWOTPlus© for each subsidiary. In situations of an oversight ministry or department of agency with oversight responsibility of multiple entities across sector clusters, there should be an ED4SP© for the oversight entity, which should be cascaded down to each of the entities within to align with the Mandate of that entity. Doing this will enhance the alignment of mandates to eliminate overlaps that can cause waste and fester conflict between entities. It is important to note that in cascading these concepts, not all the factors will be homogeneous to all subsidiaries to the same degree. As such, some differentiation will emerge.

In Chapter Six, we will be reviewing Organization Y's ED4SP© and SWOTPlus© as a sample. Thereafter, you will need to draft ED4SP© and SWOTPlus© for your own organization[s]. Also, note that Part Three is about organization[s]; thus, the decision-making and governance architecture of the organization[s] should apply. It is, therefore, the expectation that whatever your draft turns out to be, it is a personal impression that you will need to 'sell' to your management and governing body for input from others to pass it through the required governing and oversight process for consideration and approval. The process of discussing this draft for brainstorming can be facilitated by a third party, preferably an independent consultant with deep experience and appreciation of your organization's peculiarities. Therefore, all matters presented for the Organization[s] are presented based on the expectation that the executive and the non-executive board will be actively involved in this process, with the final review of an oversight body. There is no problem if you are staff within management and not a board member; knowing these requirements should help you engage your organization's leadership by sharing these insights.

6

The Concepts

Rapid business transformation has become necessary for organizations to keep up with the evolving marketplace, yet studies show that over 70 percent of large-scale transformations fail, and transformation risk remains a top concern for most organizations' leadership. More specifically, organizational leadership is the ability to lead groups of individuals toward fulfilling an organization's mission. It is a multi-faceted job requiring experience with planning, time management, an understanding of the organization's values and mission, the mastery of creating a strategic plan in line with that mission, foreseeing possible challenges in the way ahead, innovating to meet those challenges, and effectively pivoting as circumstances change.

Thus, to better understand the intricate workings of organizations and how organizations can work to achieve sustainable success in aiming for *The Africa We Want*, I created the ED4SP© Narration with Organization Y as a sample.

ED4SP© Narration With Organization Y In View As A Sample

Figure 7.0 Schematic for Organization Y ED4SP©

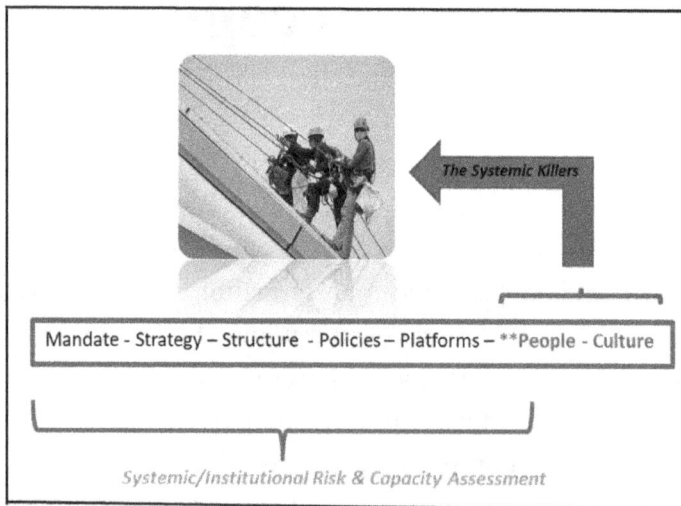

Mandate - Strategy – Structure - Policies – Platforms – **People - Culture

The Systemic Killers

Systemic/Institutional Risk & Capacity Assessment

© Newman, L.S (2021)

The Mandate: Defining Organization Y mandate will require that we think about the Group's original formation documents with its lawyers, the registrar of companies and the stock exchange in Ethiopia, and its subsidiaries in the various countries of operation as listed. Thereafter, we will need to look at the Group's strategic plans over the last decade with at least five years' statement of financial affairs for the Group and each of the subsidiaries. This will help us establish the context within which the organization[s] operate and the dynamism or resilience of the operating environments. Then, we can narrow this to its defined Mandate and markets. Rosenberg's (2020) five sector clusters were used to profile Organization Y as a private company, listed on the Addis Ababa stock exchange with operations in Ethiopia and subsidiaries in Egypt, South Africa, Senegal, the Dominican Republic of Congo [DRC], and Tanzania. Therefore, we can note that as a Group, it is positioned to serve these markets primarily and Africa in general.

The Strategy: Here, we will need to define how Organization Y will go about meeting its corporate goals in terms of overall performance, as defined in its corporate strategy and especially its Corporate Social Responsibility aspirations as a development partner to the communities and jurisdictions that it operates presently and aspires to in the near future. The key issue to note is how Organization Y's operations, products, and services advocate AfCFTA and the 17 SDGs. We also need to note Organization Y's decision to leverage partnerships with centres of excellence on various SDGs. The Group's strategic plans over the past ten years and the current period will help us recognize its strategic objectives and timelines. The five years historical statement of financial affairs will reveal how it has been funding its strategy and what level of success or otherwise is being recorded. Is the Group on track? Are all the subsidiaries on track? If no, which one[s]? Why? How can it or they be re-aligned to the Group or eliminated? What are the implications of such action between the Group with the host community and jurisdiction? Moreso, has the Group ensured a spread of subsidiaries in east, north, west, central, and south Africa with a mix of English, French, and Arab speaking jurisdictions?

The Structure: This describes how Organization Y plans to arrange the various roles in pursuit of its mandate within the Group and subsidiary structure, including external stakeholders like regulatory authorities and other agencies in its head office host jurisdiction and subsidiary host jurisdictions. It will be important, at this point, to recall Scott (2003), Gupta and Govindrajan (2004), and Addison (2004) observations to ensure Organization Y remains nimble and dynamic. Doing this will help us to notice critical relationships that we would have otherwise missed out on or not optimized. For a complex organization like Organization Y, which will likely have a matrix structure by business line, location, language, and product, I strongly suggest a stakeholder analysis tool like the Freeman (1983) Institutional Stakeholder Power and Interest Grid Analysis.

Policies: Here, we will need to consider Organization Y's founding legal documents as a Group and for the registration of each subsidiary in its host jurisdiction to get a grip of the various provisions within which Organization Y operates. After the registration documents, the governance and control arrangements as applicable to the Group and subsidiary boards and the applicable policies that relate to administration, production, storage, distribution, pricing, investments, people management, audit, and compliance are defined, carried out, assessed, and corrected. These "Policies" will help Organization Y identify the processes that it will require to legitimately, and with a sense of value, add to customers and shareholders as a private company and attain its defined strategic objectives. What rules exist to guide how these aspirations and processes are carried out at various levels of Organization Y? Tax laws, income repatriation provisions, host country industry regulations, banking provisions, and residency or indigene provisions have limitations and privileges as applicable to staffing decisions, non-compete and antitrust provisions, for instance. Organization Y will need to establish the boundaries within which it can pursue its aspirations for its competitive positioning within host communities and jurisdictions, which should, expectedly, differ in stages of market development and sophistication as well as security and political complexity.

Platforms: Here, we should take note of roles defined in Organization Y's "Structure" as discussed here and within the limitations and provisions of the "Policies" applicable to the Group and each subsidiary within its host community. Doing this will be very helpful in identifying the socio-economic needs of each subsidiary's host jurisdiction, as well as the structure of regulation and government policies, which will inform how Organization Y can get involved in its various host communities' social development projects. Such findings can flag the Platforms that Organization Y can best support in a way that compliments its business model as defined in its "Mandate".

People: This consideration is technically about making enrolment decisions. Organization Y will need to identify the type of partner organizations it will work with its internal matrix structure as defined under "Structure". How will these roles be selected, placed, elevated from outer circle to inner circle, moved around roles, monitored, and eliminated or rewarded along the journey as defined by its "Mandate" and the "Platforms" for stakeholder engagement? Having this clarified and documented, how will Organization Y deal with future successes, failures, conflicts, need for separation and replacement of key persons within its leadership while keeping its lion's gaze on its "Mandate"? Many organizations continue to experience mandate derailments and disappointments as a result of not being savvy and nimble enough or not investing in market intelligence for competitive positioning.

Culture: This is the social contract that Organization Y should have with entities listed as its "People" on how it interacts internally within the Group as a whole and within each subsidiary. Culture is a high-risk factor for mammoth structures. As such, addressing issues related to "Culture" requires delicate balancing by communication of policies and standards, as well as transparency about the basis for various key corporate decisions to avoid the grapevine's destructive tendencies against corporate cultures. How should partner organizations and governments, as defined in Organization Y's "Mandate", expect to be served? How can Organization Y receive feedback on the impact of its operations within its host communities? Clearly defining these will help enhance the efficiency of Organization Y's interventions, save running costs, and provide the synergy that Organization Y needs for leverage and systemic impact. The reverse can be the case if culture is not well defined, communicated to all parties, and clearly understood by all stakeholders. Many matrix organizations continue to experience several failed projects and eroded margins as a result of not paying particular attention to culture, as defined here, because of the magnitude of the operations.

Systemic or Institutional Risk and Capacity

Assessment: For Organization Y to adequately undertake its "Mandate" and "Strategy" as defined here, it will need independent professional services to support with derivation, assessment, and communication of its performance within each subsidiary and across the Group. Such objective assessments will be helpful for optimal stakeholder engagement. For a five-year plan, there should be a minor milestone review every two quarters or six months and each calendar year, or milestone of four quarters over the five-year period to:

(a) Review past failures for patterns and correlation and over everything.

(b) Find "what can go wrong" before they happen.

(c) What are the issues that can compromise the attainment of Organization Y's Mandate?

(d) How can they be identified, measured, and nipped in the bud?

(e) What type of mitigation measures can the group and each subsidiary deploy in its host jurisdiction?

Organization Y is a mammoth-sized organization operating in multiple jurisdictions and across the primary, secondary, and tertiary sectors, given the involvement in the extractive, agro-allied processing, and manufacturing, as well as services sector cluster in terms of logistics and merchandising across borders in Africa presents a complex organizational format. As such, the ED4SP© we just reviewed for Organization Y is a more advanced version. If your organization is relatively less complex, do not worry. The ED4SP© principles are basic and applicable across locations, ownership arrangements, sector categorizations or clusters, and organizational size or complexity.

SWOTPlus© Narration With Organization Y In View As A Sample

Figure 8.0 Schematic for Organization Y's SWOTPlus©

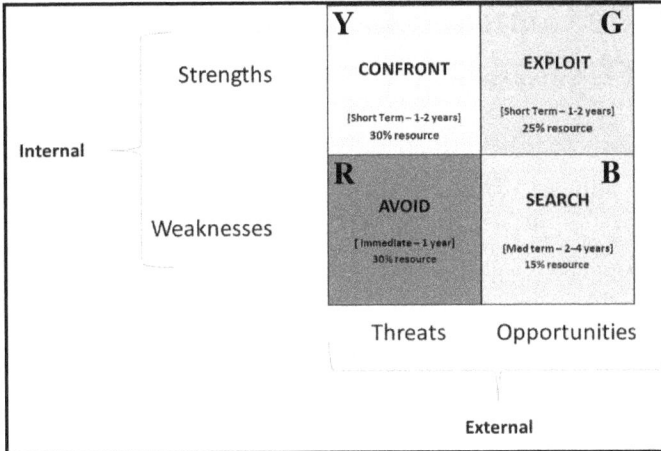

		Y		**G**
	Strengths	CONFRONT		EXPLOIT
		[Short Term – 1-2 years] 30% resource		[Short Term – 1-2 years] 25% resource
Internal		**R**		**B**
	Weaknesses	AVOID		SEARCH
		[Immediate – 1 year] 30% resource		[Med term – 2–4 years] 15% resource
		Threats		Opportunities
				External

© Newman, L.S (2021)

Application of SWOTPlus© Concept in *Figure 8.0* to Organization Y

Organization Y's strengths and weaknesses are internal within the Group and within the subsidiaries; as such, they are relatively controllable by Organization Y from decisions of the board[s] and management within the Group and each subsidiary. On the other hand, opportunities and threats are external to Organization Y and relatively uncontrollable, but the capacity to thrive and stay ahead of turbulences are enhanced with effective intelligence gathering, constructive engagements, negotiations, alliance building, leveraging of applicable networks based on validated facts and compliance with regulation and laws of host jurisdictions.

Likely Contents of the Four Quadrants for Organization Y

- **R** – What is both an internal weakness to Organization Y and an external threat to Organization Y? This is a dream killer! It must be addressed urgently to move to the Y or B zone.

- **B** – What is an internal weakness to Organization Y but has potential external opportunities to Organization Y? This is an area to invest in, find out more about, and plan a strategy to enhance internal strength and move to the Y zone.

- **Y** – What is an internal strength to Organization Y but a threat externally to Organization Y? This is a good one to be conquered and converted to a G zone for harvest.

- **G** – What is an internal strength to Organization Y and has opportunities externally for Organization Y? These are low-hanging fruits that should be harvested urgently because, depending on industry dynamism, the situation may not last!

Figure 9.0 Organization Y's SWOTPlus© for the five years Narration

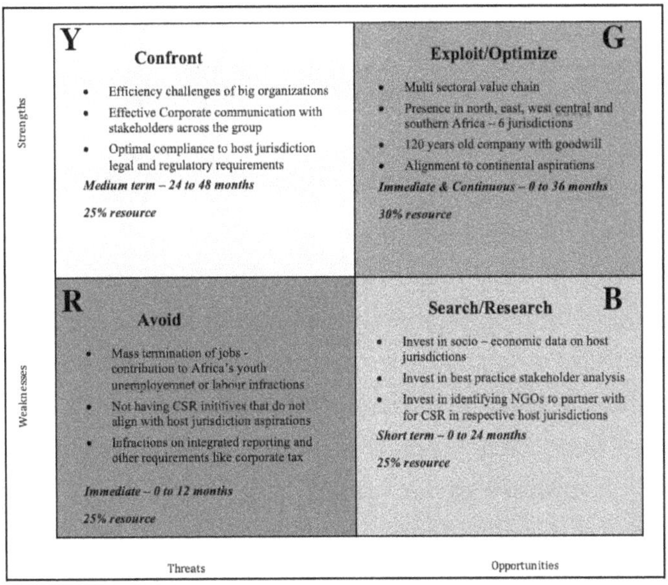

© Newman, L.S (2021)

Narration of *Figure 9.0* Organization Y SWOTplus© for the First Two Years

We are able to derive Organization Y's SWOTPlus© because the ED4SP© was well aligned. Therefore,

1. Contents of the four quadrants for Organization Y were very clear in terms of strategic focus for what to avoid, search further, confront, and exploit.

2. Clarity of entity design in descriptive terms also helped in listing out the key issues in each quadrant.

3. In view of this clarity and Organization Y's plan for the

101

Group, it is easy to set priorities for the five years. What to avoid that presents as both internal weaknesses to the Group and external threats to its "Mandate" and "Strategy" should be addressed within 0 to 12 months. All should be cleared before the close of the first year of the plan period. Areas of opportunities but weaknesses to Organization Y should be researched and ascertained within 0 to 24 months. That is, all intelligence and research, as applicable to the plan, should be completed within the first two years of the plan period to enable Organization Y to derive applicable benefits from such an investment. Areas that are both strengths and opportunities to Organization Y should be exploited or optimized within the first three years of the five years plan or before half of the plan period. Then lastly, areas of strength to Organization Y but external weaknesses in the target "Mandate" and "Strategy" space should be fully confronted within 24 to 48 months of the 60 months plan period in order to have systemic outcomes that can be measured and can help in planning the next five years on its way to the first ten years block of the Agenda 2063 aspired journey.

4. Leveraging on [4] above, Organization Y is able to allocate resources to each strategic focus area. This process will help Organization Y manage revenue, liquidity, time, and material commitment to the initiatives. The percentage of resources allocated in the first year of the plan should always add up to 100 percent.

5. With this arrangement, Organization Y will be able to see the systemic outcome of the Group's interventions in its six host jurisdictions.

6. The overall objective is to also ensure that as issues are addressed, they get moved to other zones in the two-by-two matrix. For example, when addressed, items in the R zone should move to the Y or B zone as progress. In the next plan period, items in the B zone can be in the G zone if converted to strength and still an opportunity. When confronted, items in the Y zone naturally move to the G zone, where all zones should transition by the close of the planning period.

7. Organization Y should, as risk mitigation and management matter, ensure that nothing moves from the Y, B, or G zone into the R zone by staying informed and watchful to know when to shift the Group focus.

Summary Of Organizational ED4SP© and SWOTPlus©

In chapter six, we saw how ED4SP© and SWOTPlus© could apply to an organization using Organization Y. We also saw how paying close attention to ED4SP© helps the process of applying SWOTPlus©. In the next chapter, you will have space for your reflections, and this will support you in deriving your organization's ED4SP© and

SWOTplus©, at least for your initial plan period, pending further discussions of your thoughts with your peers and oversight body in your organization. If you can share these thoughts with your organization's board, please let me know how things go. I look forward to your feedback after completion.

7

Reflections On The Concepts

In the book titled Essentialism: The Disciplined Pursuit of Less, McKeown (2014) said, *"Essentialism is a disciplined, systematic approach for determining where our highest point of contribution lies, then making execution of those things almost effortless"*. In a similar perspective, Newman (2011) cited Charan's (2009) statement in the book, Leadership In The Era of Economic Uncertainty: New Rule For Getting The Right Things Done In Difficult Times, where the author listed six essential leadership traits for hard times, which include:

(1) Honesty and credibility.

(2) The ability to inspire.

(3) Realism tempered with optimism.

(4) Real-time connection with reality.

(5) Managing with intensity.

(6) Boldness in building for the future.

Africa is transforming and based on projected growth in demographics and the impact of the AfCFTA and Agenda 2063 on the continent, African organizations and institutions are coming under intense pressure to get more involved in the socio-economic development of their host communities and jurisdictions. This pressure has increased following the observed social net deficiencies in Africa. Many governments look to corporates and institutions in Africa, especially those in the private and non-profit sectors, for support in cash and kind.

The big question is – given what we have discussed so far; what we have reviewed using Organization Y, how will your organization like to participate?

Now, you will need to draft your organizational ED4SP© and then SWOPTPlus© using the outline in Chapter Six. To get started, we need to define your organization by answering these questions as a means to a profile, as seen in Organization Y:

a. What is the name of your organization?

b. How long has it been operational?

c. Is it a private, non-profit, or public sector organization? Which industry?

d. Where is the organization located – What country, State, City, and County?

ED4SP© **Narration for** *(Organization's name)*

- Your Organization's Profile *(Obtainable from responses to a, b, c, and d)*

- Its Mandate *(Based on the profile)*

- It's Strategy *(Approach to attaining the Mandate)*

- Its Structure *(Roles required to attain its Mandate and Strategy)*

- Its Policies *(legal boundaries in which it can attain its Mandate)*

- Its Platforms *(For stakeholder engagement on Mandate and Strategy)*

- Its People *(People the organization needs – enrolling, training, assessment)*

- Its Culture *(Organization's social contract with stakeholders)*

- Its Systemic Risks and Capacity Assessments
  (Managing the red flags)

I have a few questions that I would like us to reflect on before extending the ED4SP© you just developed for your organization:

- How did you feel about the process?

- Has your organization had other CSR projects in Africa?

- How did the projects go?

- Were there challenges? What were the challenges?

- Knowing what you know now with the ED4SP© concept, what would you have done differently?

- How would applying the ED4SP© concept to these projects have impacted your organization's projects?

111

We will now proceed to guide you in extending the various components of your organization's ED4SP© into its SWOTPlus©, as applicable to your organization's ED4SP©. I hope you have enjoyed doing this, as I would like to believe you did in drafting your organization's ED4SP©.

SWOTPlus© Narration for *(Organization's name)*

Figure 10.0 SWOTPlus© for *(Organization's name)*_____ for *(state how many years)* _____ (Best to plan five years).

Y Confront	Exploit/Optimize G
• • • *Medium term – [x] to [x±n] months* *[x] % resource*	• • *Immediate –[x] to [x±n] months* *[x] resource*
R Avoid	Search/Research B
• • • *Immediate – [x] to [x±n] months* *[x]% resource*	• • • *Short term – [x] to [x±n] months* *[x]% resource*

Strengths / Weaknesses

Threats   Opportunities

You will need to visit *figure 9.0*, and its narrations to now narrate yours. Bullet points 1 to 8 on the narrations will need to apply to yours in *figure 10.0* above:

1. ....
....
....
....

2. ....
....
....
....

3. ....
....
....
....

4. ....
....
....
....

5. ....
....
,...
....

6. ....

....
....
....

7.   ....
....
....
....

8.   ....
....
....
....

Part Three Takeaways

Part Three, aptly titled "Organizations", contained two chapters which addressed a review of the two concepts ED4SP© and SWOTPlus© as well as a reflection on the concepts, based on which you developed your own ED4SP© and SWOTPlus© using observations from the pseudo–Organization Y's process as tools to proactively scope your organization's positioning for positive contribution to Africa's transformation, as emerging.

In Part Four, we will apply ED4SP© and SWOTPlus© to jurisdiction using a pseudo sample, Jurisdiction Z, to guide you in deriving your choice country as a stakeholder in *The Africa We Want*.

Part Four
Jurisdictions

AFRICAN LEADERS' TÊTE À TÊTE

"We are not only all responsible for each other's security. We are also, in some measure, responsible for each other's welfare. Global solidarity is both necessary and possible. It is necessary because without a measure of solidarity, no society can be truly stable, and no one's prosperity truly secure." – **Kofi Anan**

In September 2015, the United Nations General Assembly adopted the 2030 Agenda for Sustainable Development, which includes 17 Sustainable Development Goals (SDGs). Building on the principle of "leaving no one behind", the new Agenda emphasises a holistic approach to achieving sustainable development for all. Almost every country in the world has promised to improve the planet and the lives of its citizens by 2030. The 17 global goals, also known as the Sustainable Development Goals (SDGs), are:

(1) No poverty.

(2) Zero hunger.

(3) Good health and well-being.

(4) Quality education.

(5) Gender equality.

(6) Clean water and sanitation.

(7) Affordable and clean energy.

(8) Decent work and economic growth.

(9) Industry, innovation, and infrastructure.

(10) Reduced inequality.

(11) Sustainable cities and communities.

(12) Responsible consumption and production.

(13) Climate action.

(14) Life below water.

(15) Life on land.

(16) Peace and justice, strong institutions.

(17) Partnership to achieve the goals. [UN, March 2020].

According to the African Union, Agenda 2063 is Africa's blueprint and master plan for transforming Africa into the global powerhouse of the future. The genesis of Agenda 2063 was the realization by African leaders that there was a need to refocus and reprioritize Africa's agenda from the struggle against apartheid and the attainment of political independence for the continent, which had been the focus of the Organization of African Unity (OAU), the precursor of the African Union. The African Union now prioritized inclusive social and economic development, continental and regional integration, democratic governance, peace, and security, among other issues aimed at repositioning Africa to become a dominant player in the global arena. In furtherance of this shift in focus at the African Union, Agenda 2063 is designed to have seven Aspirational Areas and 37 Priority Areas. The seven aspirational areas are:

(1) A prosperous Africa based on inclusive growth and sustainable development.

(2) An integrated continent politically united and based on the ideals of Pan Africanism and the vision of the African Renaissance.

117

(3) An Africa of good governance, democracy, respect for human rights, justice and the rule of law.

(4) A peaceful and secure Africa.

(5) Africa with a strong cultural identity, common heritage, values, and ethics.

(6) An Africa whose development is people-driven, relying on the potential offered by African people, especially its women and youth, and caring for children.

(7) An Africa known as a strong, united, resilient, and influential global player and partner.

For ease of implementation, the Agenda 2063 Plan is split into five blocks of progressive ten years or a decade. The First Ten-Year Implementation Plan (FTYIP) of Agenda 2063 (2013 – 2023) is the first in a series of five ten-year plans. The FTYIP enumerates 20 thematic areas of the Agenda 2063 goals, linked to the seven Aspirations and 37 Priority areas. These are to be implemented at a national level by jurisdiction among African countries.

According to Wikipedia, the African Continental Free Trade Area (AfCFTA) is a free trade area created by the African Continental Free Trade Agreement among African nations. Based on this agreement, AfCFTA became the largest in the world by the number of participating countries since the formation of the World Trade Organization. The general objectives of the agreement are to:

(a) Create a single market, deepening the economic integration of the continent.

(b) Establish a liberalised market through multiple rounds of negotiations.

(c) Aid the movement of capital and people, facilitating investment.

(d) Move towards the establishment of a future continental customs union.

(e) Achieve sustainable and inclusive socio-economic development, gender equality, and structural transformations within member states.

(f) Enhance the competitiveness of member states within Africa and in the global market.

(g) Encourage industrial development through diversification and regional value chain development, agricultural development, and food security.

(h) Resolve challenges of multiple and overlapping memberships.

In Chapter One of this body of work, we noted the trajectories for Africa with the paradox of being a naturally endowed continent yet challenged in the conversion of such natural endowment into wealth for its people; thus, Africa remains technically the poorest continent on earth, in terms of per capita and human development indices. At this point, I would like to share one of late Madiba Nelson Mandela's quotes, *"Overcoming poverty is not a task of char-*

ity, it is an act of justice. Like slavery and apartheid, poverty is not natural. It is man-made, and it can be overcome and eradicated by the actions of human beings".

In view of this contextual background and in the spirit of *Ubuntu*, the big questions for us in Part Four will likely be:

[a] How can an African jurisdiction enhance its contribution to the aspired African transformation?

[b] How can a jurisdiction apply the ED4SP© and SWOTPlus© concepts to positively impact systemic outcomes in small but consistent ways?

If you are an African in diaspora, a government official at any level of government (national, sub-national, sector) within your country in Africa, an African with aspirations for political office, or an international civil servant in the development space working with a multilateral agency supporting Africa, or a scholar with a particular interest in Africa affiliated with any of the administrative roles within the five regional block in Africa. In that case, I welcome you to this discussion. As earlier indicated, this is a highly simplified discussion, between the reader and the author, about the practical application of two concepts; hence, I will not be going into any theories of development, or international relations, or government.

Therefore, I would like to start by walking us through the ED4SP© concept as applicable to jurisdictions using a pseudo-Jurisdiction Z and then, based on this sample, walk you through developing your country's ED4SP©. Thereafter, we will also review the SWOTPlus© for our sample jurisdiction so that you can develop yours. If we do this right, you should be able to clearly see what is most important to your jurisdiction[s]. Figure 11.0 is the schematic that we will use for Jurisdiction Z ED4SP©, and *Figure 12.0* is the schematic that we will use for Jurisdiction Z SWOTPlus©. We need to develop a profile for our pseudo jurisdiction to get started.

Psuedo Jurisdiction Z Profile

Our pseudo jurisdiction in Part Four is Jurisdiction Z, which for reasons of this process, we will assume that it is a former Portuguese colony that gained its independence in 1960. Jurisdiction Z is a Southern African Country and a member of the Southern African Development Community [SADC]. According to Wikipedia, the Southern African Development Community is an inter-governmental organisation headquartered in Gaborone, Botswana. Its goal is to further regional socio-economic cooperation and integration as well as political and security cooperation among 16 countries in southern Africa. The SADC is one of the five sub-regional blocs within the AU. The SADC Free Trade Area was established in August 2008, after the implementation of the SADC Protocol on Trade in 2000 laid the foundation for its formation. In view of the background, Jurisdiction Z is set to extend this experience into wider Africa via the AfCFTA.

121

Jurisdiction Z has a population of 21 million, spread across 4 Provinces that make up 26 Municipalities and 301 communities. It is a largely agrarian economy, with 75 percent of its population living in rural communities. Jurisdiction Z diaspora population is about 10 percent of its population and is mainly spread across Europe. About 55 percent of the population lives below $2 a day, the youth unemployment rate is 52 percent, and the school dropout rate is 40 percent due to various factors, including childhood pregnancies and early customary marriage. The last census was 15 years ago, and its constitution was last reviewed in 1990. Jurisdiction Z is inland and has no direct access to the seaports. Jurisdiction Z is a democratic country that runs a hybrid constitutional system with a general election every four years; its mineral resources include copper, iron ore, aluminum, and gold. Agricultural resources include timber, cashew, cotton, and tea.

We will review Jurisdiction Z ED4SP© and SWOTPlus© as a sample. Later, in Part Four, you will be guided to draft your jurisdiction's ED4SP© and SWOTPlus©. It is also important to note that the expectation is that whatever your draft turns out to be, it is a personal impression that you will need to "sell" to your stakeholders and the applicable oversight process for consideration. If you are a leader at the national or sub-national level, please know that these principles and processes are scalable and can be spun to suit many situations.

8

The Concepts

The concepts here refer to jurisdiction, a country or territory with constitutional power to make lawful decisions and judgments. Simply put, it is the geographic boundary an entity can operate in or act over based on the constitution of that territory. The constitution provides the framework for governing the country or territory and protecting the rights of its citizens and other individuals or organisations legally operating in that territory. All jurisdictions strive to achieve a set of broad social goals, including economic efficiency, growth, freedom, equity, stability, and security. How successful a jurisdiction is at attaining these goals influences the quality of life of all its people. For such economic solidity, jurisdictions have laws that provide customs-related advantages and exemptions from national and sub-national taxations and duties, thus, offering individuals and organisations constitutional trade conditions expected to be favourable and a liberal regulatory environment to operate their businesses. This aims to attract foreign investments, collaborations, and organisations that can facilitate entry into the world marketplace for some of the nation's goods and services, thereby generating employment and, at the same time, foreign exchange for the country or territory.

Here, we will bring conceptual clarity to jurisdiction by looking at the concepts and how they can help support the attainment of *"The Africa we want"* using Jurisdiction Z as a sample.

ED4SP© Narration With
Jurisdiction Z In View As A Sample

Figure 11.0 Schematic for Jurisdiction Z ED4SP©

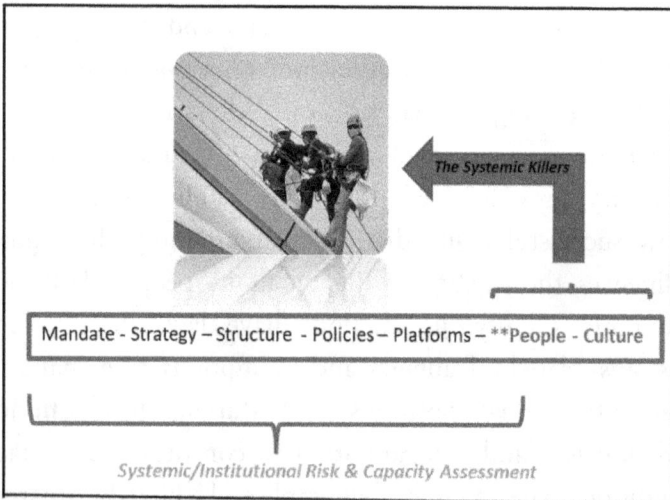

© Newman, L.S (2021)

The Mandate: The Constitution is the reference material for the mandate as applicable to jurisdiction because it is from the constitution that all component parts of a state and its sub-nationals derive their existence. The constitution provides the framework for the governance of a country, and it is critical to protecting the rights of everyone because it sets the framework for how laws are made and the government operates. At this point, it is important that we recollect that Africa, the world's second largest and second-most-populous continent, after Asia in both cases, is NOT a Country. African nations cooperate through the establishment of the African Union (AU), a continental union consisting of 55 member states located on the continent of Africa, with headquarters in Addis Ababa, Ethiopia. Chapter One provided a full context on Africa, and at this point, it is advisable that we revisit Chapter One for continental context, within which we derive our pseudo jurisdiction – Jurisdiction Z.

The Strategy: Here, we will need to review the national plan for Jurisdiction Z. A national plan is a long-term plan for the development of a national economy. Various countries have five-to-ten-year plans, while others have three-year rolling plans or two cycles of five-year plans for a decade of planning. In Chapter One, we flagged one of Africa's challenges – long-term planning and commitment to such, unlike the Asian countries. In view of this, Agenda 2063: The Africa We Want has been lauded. In the case of Jurisdiction Z, the national plan should address the national situation and needs relative to the 17 SDGs and Jurisdiction Z's alignment with Agenda 2063 seven focus areas and its readiness for AfCFTA. The national plan should be backed by valid data. For Jurisdiction Z, a largely agrarian economy, the growth of the progressive sectors to enhance the output of the primary sector cluster may be a critical strategic aspiration, given its largely extractive economy.

The Structure: This describes how the various levels of government in Jurisdiction Z will be governed, show accountability, and be controlled by the people of Jurisdiction Z. The levels of government include the national (executive, legislative, and judiciary) and sub-national (state and local government). Had Jurisdiction Z been a parliamentary system, the stricture would have been national (federal and regional) with sub-national (province, municipalities, and communities). Some jurisdictions, like Jurisdiction Z, have a hybrid system that is customised to their situations as linked to their history. The role of the private sector, public sector, social sector, ministries, departments, and agencies should be defined by acts. The big question here is whether these agencies' mandates complement the national plan and if the national plan is aligned to continental and sub-regional roles in a matrix format. This will be critical to Jurisdiction Z's success at the 17 SDGs and the seven focus areas for Agenda 2063.

Policies: This relates to applicable laws and charters for respective roles in the "Structure". For this to be effective, the constitutional powers must be apt, understood, and in practice. Uncertainty in policy directions is bad for jurisdictions because it affects planning and triggers artificial defence mechanisms from the various agencies within and outside the "Structure". The policies should enable and continually improve separation of powers, checks and balances, judicial autonomy and independence of specialised institutions.

Platforms: Here, we should take note of roles defined in Jurisdiction Z's "Structure" as discussed here and within the limitations and provisions of the "Policies" applicable to the country and each sub-national level to identify performance challenges within each sub-national level, especially the socio-economic needs within each community. Platforms, including statutory meetings of the various roles in the "Structure", at all national and sub-national levels for engagement with all sectoral cluster administrators, are healthy necessities. The roles of the public, private, social, non-governmental, and civil society organizations should be listed and included at all public sessions as applicable to law-making, community conflict resolution, budgeting, and planning, as well as performance reporting.

People: This consideration is technically about making enrolment decisions. Jurisdiction Z will need to identify the sub nationals, ministries, departments, and agencies required by each of the 17 SDGs and Agenda 2063 thematic areas in a matrix arrangement. How will these entities be selected, enrolled, progressed, monitored, and eliminated or rewarded along the journey as defined by Jurisdiction Z's constitution and the "Platforms" for engagement? Many African countries have challenges with platforms for civil engagement with society and receiving feedback from the citizenry; thus, the source of many agitations. The lion's gaze for Jurisdiction Z should be grassroots engagement, leveraging the sub-national levels, with inclusivity and diversity to communicate and sell the vision for progressing the sectoral clusters to more sophistication for increased value add and socio-economic impact. Because of the short-termism of politics linking national decisions to election cycles, plan derailment is not an option in a democratic setting that aspires to grow in the current dispensation on the continent.

Culture: This is the social contract that Jurisdiction Z should have with its citizens and residents. The constitution must be clear on the rights and responsibilities of citizens and residents, as well as the obligations of the government to the people at the national and sub-national levels. For Jurisdiction Z, the national anthem, and the national pledge of allegiance, included in the constitution with civil and criminal law provisions, set the tone. Thus, the critical roles of the Judiciary and the sub-nationals to the communities and traditional systems for behavioural conformity. Culture is a high-risk factor for jurisdictions in transition, like Jurisdiction Z – all need to be on the same page, and the leadership must clearly articulate an inspiring future, as well as show commitment to that journey with a listening ear towards various segments of society. The role of a thriving and engaged civil society and non-governmental organizations, the police force, and the traditional system is important.

Systemic or Institutional Risk and Capacity Assessment: For Jurisdiction Z to adequately live by the provisions of its constitution and national plans as defined in "Mandate" and "Strategy", it will need thriving and well-aligned independent and specialized institutions such as the Accountant General's Office, the National Office of Statistics, the Attorney General's Office, the Judicial Council, Anti-crimes Commission, the Law and Drug Enforcement Commission, the Independent Electoral Commission, Central Bank, the Public Defender, the Police Commission, State Security Services, Ministry of Defense and the National Population Commission. These independent institutions are critical to derivation, assessment, analysis, and periodic reporting on issues, while others offer mitigation interventions that may be needed to keep the status quo as well as nip potentially volatile issues in the bud.

Likely challenges to be faced by Jurisdiction Z, being a SADC member, findings indicate these may include social, development, economic, trade, education, health, diplomatic, defence, security, and political challenges.

The socio-economic, political, and security cooperation aims of SADC are equally wide-ranging and intended to address the various common challenges. Jurisdiction Z is, therefore, well positioned as a member of SADC and within the strategic aspirations of the AU.

In terms of jurisdictions, the ED4SP© we just reviewed for Jurisdiction Z is applicable to a single jurisdiction. However, the same can be done for SADC or any of the other four sub-regional blocs as may be required, using the same principles.

SWOTPlus© Narration With Jurisdiction Z In View As A Sample

Figure 12.0 Schematic for Jurisdiction Z's SWOTPlus©

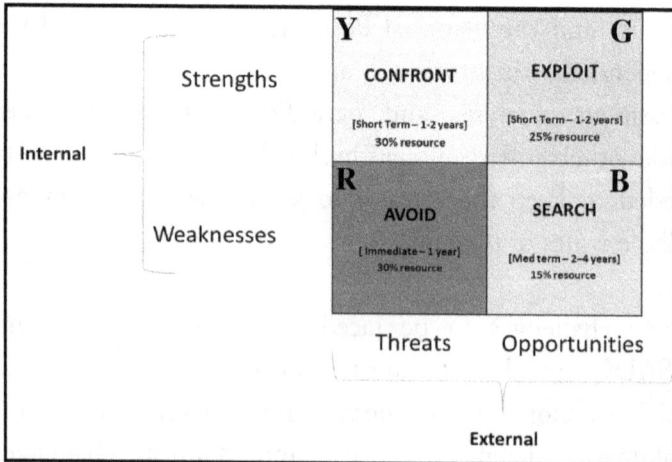

Application of SWOTPlus© Concept
In *Figure 12.0* to Jurisdiction Z

Jurisdiction Z's strengths and weaknesses are internal to Jurisdiction Z. On the other hand, opportunities and threats are external to Jurisdiction Z and relatively uncontrollable, but the capacity to thrive and stay ahead of turbulences is enhanced with an effective constitution, clearly articulated national plans, intelligence gathering, constructive engagements, negotiations, alliance building, leveraging applicable sub-regional and continental networks, based on validated facts and compliance with the provisions of its own constitution.

Likely Contents of the Four Quadrants
for Jurisdiction Z

- **R** – What is both an internal weakness to Jurisdiction Z and an external threat to Jurisdiction Z? This is a killer! This must be addressed urgently to move to the Y or B zone.

- **B** – What is an internal weakness to Jurisdiction Z but has external potential opportunities to Jurisdiction Z? This is an area to invest in, find out more about, and plan a strategy to enhance internal strength and move to the Y zone.

- **Y** – What is an internal strength to Jurisdiction Z but a threat externally to Jurisdiction Z? This is a good one to be conquered and converted to a G zone for harvest.

- **G** – What is an internal strength to Jurisdiction Z and has opportunities externally for Jurisdiction Z? These are low-hanging fruits that should be harvested urgently because, depending on industry dynamism, the situation may not last!

Figure 13.0 Schematic for Jurisdiction Z's SWOTPlus©

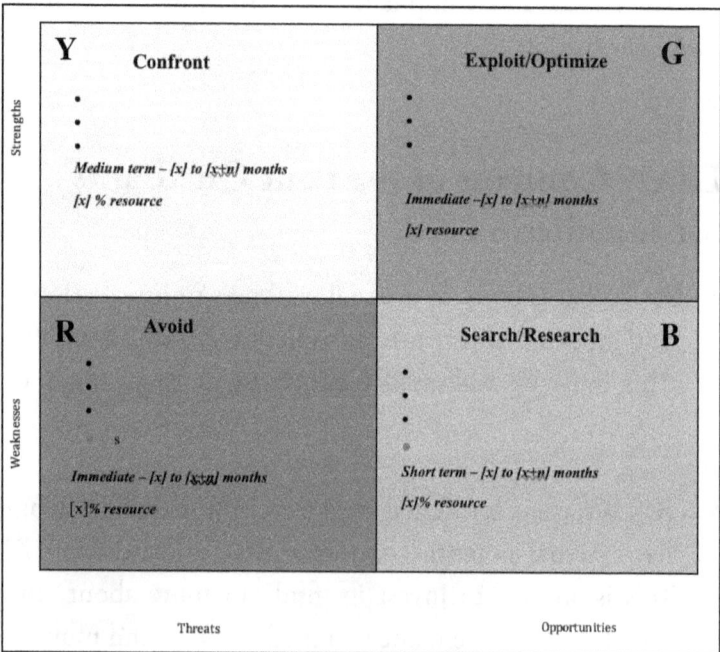

	Y Confront	Exploit/Optimize **G**
Strengths	• • • Medium term – [x] to [x±n] months [x] % resource	• • • Immediate –[x] to [x±n] months [x] resource
Weaknesses	**R** Avoid • • • s Immediate – [x] to [x±n] months [x]% resource	Search/Research **B** • • • Short term – [x] to [x±n] months [x]% resource
	Threats	Opportunities

© Newman, L.S (2021)

Narration of *Figure 13.0* Jurisdiction Z SWOTPlus© for the First Five Years

We are able to derive Jurisdiction Z's SWOTPlus© because the ED4SP© was well-aligned. Therefore,

1. Contents of the four quadrants for Jurisdiction Z were very clear in terms of strategic focus for what to avoid, search further, confront, and exploit.

2. Clarity of entity design in descriptive terms also helped in listing out the key issues in each quadrant.

3. In view of this clarity and Jurisdiction Z's national situation as reviewed in the ED4SP©, it is easy to set priorities for the five years. What to avoid that are both internal weaknesses to Jurisdiction Z and external threats to its constitution and national plan, as referenced in the "Mandate" and "Strategy" section of the ED4SP© should be addressed within 0 to 12 months. All should be cleared before the close of the first year of the five-year plan period. However, Jurisdiction Z will need to keep vigilance on these issues all through the plan period. Areas of opportunities but weakness to Jurisdiction Z should be researched and ascertained within 0 to 12 months of the plan shelf life. That is, all intelligence and research, as applicable to the plan, should be completed within the first year of the plan period to enable Jurisdiction Z to derive applicable benefits from such an investment. Areas that are both strengths to Jurisdiction Z and opportunities should be exploited or

133

optimised within the first three years of the five-year plan or before half of the plan period. Then lastly, areas of strength to Jurisdiction Z but external weaknesses in the target Mandate and Strategy space should be fully confronted within 24 to 60 months of the plan period in order to have systemic outcomes that can be measured and can help in planning the next five years on our way to the first ten years block of the Agenda 2063 aspired journey.

4. Leveraging on [4] above, Jurisdiction Z is able to make resources available to each strategic focus area, which should be translated into the annual national budgets in the proportions indicated for applicable years. This process will help Jurisdiction Z manage Internally Generated Revenue [IGR], Capital Expenditures, time, and material commitment to the initiatives.

5. With this arrangement, Jurisdiction Z will be able to see the systemic outcome of the interventions via the National Office of Statistics.

6. The overall objective is also to ensure that as issues are addressed, they get to be moved into other areas. For example, when addressed, items in the R zone should move to the Y or B zone. In the next plan period, items in the B zone can be in the G zone if converted to strength and still an opportunity. When confronted, items in the Y zone naturally move to the G zone.

7. Jurisdiction Z should ensure that nothing moves from

the Y, B, or G zone into the R zone by staying informed and watchful to know when to shift the country's focus. Thus, the importance of Jurisdiction Z leaders remaining engaged.

Summary of Jurisdictional ED4SP© and SWOTPlus©

In Chapter Eight, we saw how ED4SP© and SWOTPlus© could apply to a Jurisdiction or Jurisdiction Cluster using Jurisdiction Z. We also saw how a well-developed ED4SP© could enhance the process of developing a SWOTPlus©. In Chapter Nine, I will guide you in the development of an ED4SP© and SWOTPlus© for the jurisdiction of your choice or for a cluster of jurisdictions.

9
Reflections On
The Concepts

Building on progress so far recorded since the SDGs and Agenda 2063 came into existence; several countries are already taking steps to translate the ambitions articulated in the 2030 Agenda into tangible outcomes for their people; they are beginning by integrating the SDGs into their national visions and plans. All these are highly transformative for Africa and applauded! However, the big questions are:

[a] How can you avoid the policies and practices slowing Africa's ability to innovate more and promote critical thinking at the grassroots level?

[b] Given what we have discussed so far and what we have reviewed using Jurisdiction Z, how will you like to proceed for your jurisdiction or cluster of jurisdictions?

Now, you will need to draft an ED4SP© and then SWOPTPlus© for your chosen jurisdiction. If you are an

African leader or an African in diaspora and would like to use the concepts to sketch your aspired country to know how you can best support, either as a policy advisor, a volunteer national builder, or a consultant offering advisory, I look forward to your outcome!

ED4SP© Narration for *(Name of Jurisdiction[s])*

• My Jurisdictions Profile *(Leverage Jurisdiction Z description)*

- Its Mandate *(Based on the profile and constitution)*

- It's Strategy *(Based on national plan)*

- Its Structure *(National and sub-national and specialized institutions)*

- Its Policies *(Legal provisions and gazettes)*

- Its Platforms *(For stakeholder engagement on Mandate and Strategy)*

- Its People *(Entities in Structure and provisions in law on Mandates)*

- Its Culture *(Interaction at national, sub-national, and other levels)*

```



```

- Its Systemic Risks and Capacity Assessments *(Specialized institutions)*

```



```

We will now proceed to guide you in extending the various components of your jurisdiction's ED4SP© into its SWOTPlus©, as applicable to your jurisdiction's ED4SP©.

SWOTPlus© Narration for *(Jurisdiction's name)*

Figure 14.0 SWOTPlus© for *(Name of Jurisdiction)*_____
_____ for *(state how many years)* _____
(Best to plan 5 years).

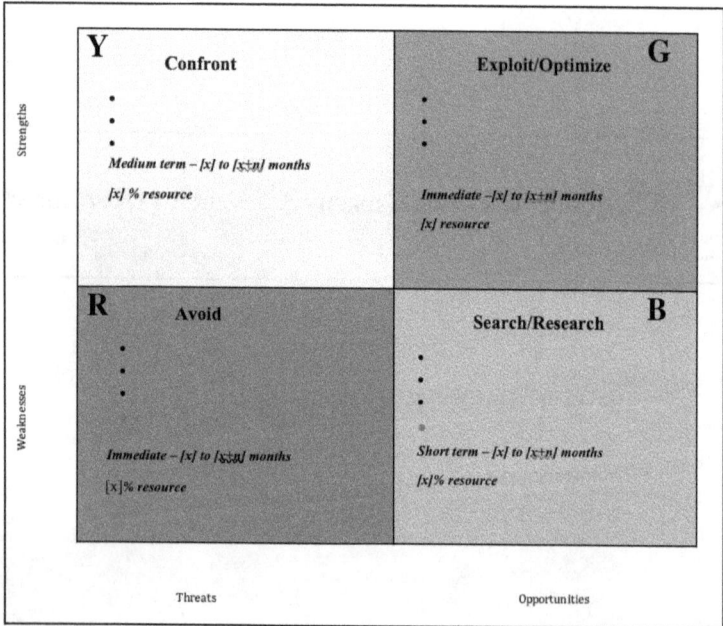

© Newman, L.S (2021)

You will need to visit *figure 13.0*, and its narrations to now narrate yours. Bullet points 1 to 8 on the narrations will need to apply to yours in *figure 14.0* above:

1. ....
....
....
....

2. ....
....
....
....

3. ....
....
....
....

4. ....
....
....
....

5. ....
....
....
....

6. ....
....
....
....

7. ....

....

....

....

8. ....

....

....

....

Part Four Takeaways

Part Four, aptly titled Jurisdiction, contained two chapters which reviewed the ED4SP© and SWOTPlus© concepts using a pseudo–Jurisdiction Z and extended the issues discussed to facilitate your process of deriving your own jurisdictional sample, as promised. I thank you for the time you invested in these discussions.

Now, it's time for Part Five, the final part of *African Leaders' Tête À Tête*, titled "The Momentum", which is, technically, a call to action applicable to the Individual, Organizations, and Jurisdictions. I kindly invite you to join me as we encourage one another to take the next step. Hopefully, the second block of the ten-year plan for Agenda 2063: *"The Africa We Want"*, will find us ready to move into our deliberately derived place as an individual, organization, or jurisdiction.

PART FIVE
The Momentum

"In brief, leaders with motive and power bases tap followers' motives in order to realize the purposes of both leaders and followers." – **James MacGregor Burns.**

The concept of transformational leadership was initially introduced by leadership expert and presidential biographer James MacGregor Burns. According to Burns, transformational leadership can be seen when *"leaders and followers make each other advance to a higher level of moral and motivation."* Through the strength of their vision and personality, transformational leaders are able to inspire followers to change expectations, perceptions, and motivations to work towards common goals. Later, researcher, Bernard M. Bass, expanded upon Burns' original ideas to develop what is today referred to as Bass' Transformational Leadership Theory. According to Bass, transformational leadership can be defined based on its impact on followers. Transformational leaders, Bass suggested, garner trust, respect, and admiration from their followers. In other words, transformational leaders are charismatic; they transform dreams into reality. In Chapter One, we reviewed Africa as a continent. From that review, we can adequately infer that Africa is on a trajectory. The path is well defined, the collective aspiration resonates, and islands of progress are emerging.

However, the speed could be better if there is more alignment. Africa has many topside opportunities – the youngest continent, home to 10 out of 20 fastest growing economies in the world and naturally endowed. Poverty, insecurity, challenges from climate change, observed sub-optimal governance practices, and other challenges can be flipped into opportunities or socio-economic explosives if left to fester. The African Union provides a unifying platform for envisioning, drawing consensus and support, despite its own institutional challenges. Thus, the requirement for us to reinforce that platform by individually contributing in structured and balanced ways as individuals, organizations, and jurisdictions. *African Leaders' Tête À Tête* aspires to make a small contribution in that direction via this publication. In the introductory section, I provided insights into how our discussion will go and to what end. Now it is time for us to gain momentum on what we have covered in the preceding nine chapters to the objectives for our discussion.

The Merriam-Webster Dictionary defined the term "momentum" as *"a property of a moving body that the body has by virtue of its mass and motion, and that is equal to the product of the body's mass and velocity broadly"*. I am a strong advocate of Africa and Africans putting our heads together in the spirit of "Ubuntu" to ensure that we keep Africa's development moving on a positive and progressive trajectory, hopefully at a pace equal to or faster than the rest of the world. This is most important, given the observable paradox of Africa being naturally endowed, yet comparatively the poorest continent, with a burgeoning youthful population. I personally think our combined growth rate

147

needs to double the projected global growth rate at any point.

As earlier indicated, some of the questions many leaders have asked me over the latter two decades of my career include:

[a] How can one put all aspects of my organization in a compressed and simplified manner to show balance?

[b] How do I prioritize and allocate resources to competing strategic initiatives?

[c] I will not be in my role endlessly, so how can I make a meaningful contribution with systemic outcomes?

With ED4SP© and SWOTPlus©, *African Leaders' Tête À Tête* has been a discussion between the author and three main spheres of leadership with potential impact in Africa. In furtherance of this, we have discussed ED4SP© and SWOTPlus© as applicable to:

[a] Individual leaders with aspiration for self-application of the concepts for personal application.

[b] Corporate leaders with primary, secondary, or tertiary responsibility for entities that include corporate organizations, institutions, government ministries, departments, and agencies.

[c] Leaders with jurisdictional and jurisdictional cluster leadership responsibilities.

We will conclude by listing critical steps for momentum to our aspired collective future in *The Africa We Want*.

General Guide:

- All items in the R and B quadrants of SWOTPlus© need to be reviewed, and tentative action plans drawn to address them as a first priority.

- Thereafter, all items in the G quadrant should be noted as low-hanging fruits.

In terms of progression, as items in the R section in the quadrant of SWOTPlus© are being implemented successfully, and the items in the B quadrant are initiated, while items in the G area are harvested as low-hanging fruits, the general observation is that the issues in the Y section tend to progress into G section as new low-hanging fruits in the next planning phase.

In terms of ED4SP©, all eight components must be completely thought through with full details of each item to ensure the ED4SP© is balanced before initiating items in the G quadrant of your SWOTPlus© as an individual, organization, or jurisdiction.

Individual: Firstly, decide on the eight components of ED4SP©, followed by allocation of resources available and within your control. Secondly, decide if it is a solo project or collaboration, and how and in which location and sector. Start small; you can always scale up. And network, network, network. Then, when comfortable, share your project with your network; your project may just be an answer to someone's hopes and aspirations. Lastly, African leaders now engage the diaspora; however, it has been an unbalanced engagement because many African countries do not have the infrastructure for diaspora voting. It is important that African diaspora networks lobby the AU ahead of the next ten years of Agenda 2063 to ensure the inclusion of continental infrastructure to facilitate diaspora participation in their respective home country elections as part of inclusion, given the role African diaspora is expected to play in Africa's transformation as defined.

Organizations: Firstly, confirm the time available for you with the organization. It is important to ascertain how long you have left with the organization and plan your succession internally on the initiative so that your plan indicates that as you present your initiative. Start as a pilot and scale up. Ensure it gets up to the Board and a decision is taken about it. Manage expectations and plan resources. Then, consider regulatory consent and collaborate with like-minded organizations. Think scale. In view of the potential impact of AfCFTA, African countries need to be encouraged to create National Governance Codes for the private, public, and social or non-profit that allow for scaled codes for the small, medium, and large corporates. Effective governance practices and stable macroeconomic environments tend to attract required medium to long-term capital for high-impact investments.

Jurisdiction[s]: Firstly, think data. How valid and recent are the national census data and other socio-economic information? Planning without verifiable data is futile. Then, how recent is the constitutional amendment? Has there been any constitutional amendment or economic re-alignment since the commencement of Agenda 2063? If not, then it is likely that the economic arrangement and applicable institutions may not be positioned to support continental initiatives like the AfCFTA or Agenda 2063.

The big question is – how possible is it for the AU to consider a time schedule for its members to create updated demographic databases and update economic arrangements and constitutions to align with these monumental continental arrangements? Travelling across Africa can be a major nightmare due to suboptimally connected road networks, trains, and air routes that tend to limit travellers' choices, resulting in cancellations and avoidable delays. Travelling from Lagos to Windhoek, or Lagos to Conakry or Lagos to Banjul and Senegal can last as many hours as Lagos to the US or Canada. It shouldn't be like this in an AfCFTA era.

Another big question is – how many Africans know that the African Union has a beautiful flag and an inspiring African Anthem? How many African countries fly their national flag side by side with the African Union flag and play their national anthem simultaneously with the African Union Anthem? I have, on many occasions, brought up this issue and, to my shock, realized that many African leaders, especially in corporate Africa, are not even aware that the African Union has a flag and an Anthem!

Part Five Takeaways

Part Five, aptly titled *"The Momentum"*, is compact and seeks to raise issues that can restrain the attainment of the aspirations for Agenda 2063 if not included in the second ten-year bloc plan. My expectation is that these will trigger higher-level questions ahead of the next planning period for Agenda 2063. The five big issues are:

[a] Diaspora voting in home country elections.

[b] Creation of national corporate governance codes that cater for private, public, and social or non-profit sectors as applicable to small, medium, and large corporations as a pervasive practice in all AU member jurisdictions.

[c] The need for all AU member countries to update their constitutions and undertake economic re-arrangements to facilitate alignment with and pervasive attainment of AfCFTA and Agenda 2063 aspirations.

[d] Africa, connecting with Africa – the need to urgently improve connections between major African productive and commercial hubs by road, train, air, and waterways, to ensure improved movement of people, goods and services as required for a thriving AfCFTA.

[e] Data is the new gold – Africa needs valid demographic data for planning and tracking the effects of Agenda 2063 and other initiatives. Valid and verifiable demographic data is required at sub-national, national, sub-regional, and continental levels. The African Union should consider requesting its members to, as a basic requirement, have a valid and verifiable census every decade.

If these can be considered in the next ten-year phase of Agenda 2063, and then individual leaders, organizations, and jurisdictions can explore ED4SP© and SWOTPlus© as tools for entity design and prioritization of initiatives for systemic outcomes, then the objectives of "*African Leaders' Tête À Tête: Navigating Entity Design and Prioritization For Systemic Outcomes*" would have been attained.

On this note, thank you for the time you invested in this discussion. It has been a profoundly inspiring and cherished honour to have had the privilege of your attention for this duration, and I hope the time spent has also been valuable for you. I wish you and your team[s] well with your takeaways from this discussion, and I look forward to hearing from you. As earlier indicated, I am just an email away. May we find many more opportunities to contribute to bringing forth Agenda 2063: *The Africa We Want!*

Bibliography

Addison, M. R. (2004, July). Performance Architecture: A Performance Improvement Model. *Performance Improvement.* International Society of Performance Improvement: Silver Spring, 43(6), p. 14. Alijfri, Collins & Pones (2003).

Bass, B. (1997). Does The Transactional-Transformational Leadership Paradigm Transcend Oganizational and National Boundaries? *American Psychologist* 52 (2) 130-139.

Burns, J. M. (2003). Transforming Leadership: A New Pursuit of Happiness. NY: Atlantic Monthly Press.

Bass, B.M. & Stogdill, R. M. (1990). Handbook of Leadership: Theory, Research & Managerial Applications. New York: The Free Press.

Bertalanffy, L. V. (1972, December). The History and Status of General Systems Theory. Academy of Management Journal, 407-426.

Diamonds, P.H., & Kotler, S. (2012). *Abundance: The Future Is Better Than You Think.* New York: Free Press.

Gallo, C (2016). *The Storyteller's Secret: How TED Speakers and Inspirational Leaders Turn Their Passion Into Performance.* London. St. Martin's Press. Macmillan.

Gupta, A. K., & Govindarajan, V. (2004). *Global Strategy and Organization*. New York: John Wiley & Sons.

Hayatu-Deen, M. (2002, December). *Nigeria: A challenge of building Africa's Leading Economy*. Paper presented at the annual lecture of Ahmadu Bello Allumni Association, Lagos zone. Lagos. Nigeria.

Kajunju, A. (November, 2013). Africa's Secret Weapon: The Diaspora. Special to CNN. Retrieved June 24, 2022 from https://edition.cnn.com/2013/11/01/opinion/africas -secret-weapon-diaspora/index.html

Kaufman, R. (2006). Mega Planning and Thinking: Defining and Achieving Measurable Success. In Pershing, J. A. (2006). *Handbook of Human Performance Technology. (3rd Edition)*. (pp. 139 – 154). *International Society for Performance Improvement*. San Francisco, USA. Pfeiffer.

Lacy, P., Long, J., & Spindler, W. (2020). The Circular Economy Handbook: Realizing The   Circular Advantage. United Kingdom: Palgrave Macmillan.

Newman, L. S. (2021). Africa's Current Status: The Required Alignment. A paper presented at the Virtual Second Symposium on Economics of Ignorance, a program of Hale Associates Center https://halecenter.org/event -4450625

Newman, L. S. (2020). *Storytelling: An African Leadership Journey of Performance Improvement Innovation*. In Van Tiem,

D. M., & Burns, N. C. (Eds.), Cases on Performance Improvement Innovation (pp. 126-155). IGI Global. http://doi:10.4018/978-1-7998-3673-5.ch008

Newman, L.S (2020). *Corporate Governance and Performance Imperatives for Directors in Africa: SDGs, AfCFTA and Agenda 2063.* The Director, a Magazine of the Institute of Directors Nigeria. Issue No. 24; Pages 64-71.

Newman, L.S (2019). *Leveraging Corporate Governance for Economic Development: Imperatives for Governments and Regulators in Sub Saharan Africa.* The Director, a Magazine of the Institute of Directors Nigeria. Issue No. 22, Pages: 37-48.

Newman, L. S (2011). *Transformational Leadership; A Leadership approach for changing Times.* A paper published in the FITC Journal of Banking and Finance, Vol. 2 No, 2011; pp 03-17.

Newman, L.S (2009). *The CEO's Triple Dilemma of Compensation, Employee, and Corporate Performance,* being a one-chapter manuscript along with 9 other authors in the book, "The Refractive Thinker: An Anthology of Higher Learning" published by the Lentz Leadership Institute of Las Vegas, Nevada, USA. ISBN 978-9823036-0-3. Spring 2009.

Newman, L. S (August, 2007). *Emerging HR Landmines: Critical Concerns for CEOs.* Being an article published the Business Day Daily Newspaper, Thursday August 30, 2007.

Newman, L.S (February, 2007). *The CEOs Dual Dilemma: Governance & Sustainability In An Increasingly Dynamic Global Business Environment*. Being an article published on the Business Day Daily Newspaper of Monday February 19, 2007.

McKeown, G. (2014). Essentialism: The Disciplined Pursuit of Less. New York: Crown Business.

Nossel, M. (2018). Powered by Storytelling: Excavate, Craft and Present Stories to Transform Business Communication. New York, USA. McGraw-Hill Books.

Rosenberg, M. (January, 2020). 5 Sectors of The Economy. Retrieved July 19, 2022 from https://www.thoughtco.com/sectors-of-the-economy-1435795

Scott, W. R. (2003). *Organizations: Rational, Natural, and Open Systems* (5th ed.). Upper Saddle River, NJ: Prentice Hall.

United Nations. (2020). Sustainable Development Goals. Retrieved March 27, 2020 from https://sustainable development.un.org/?menu=1300

Wren, D. A. (1994). *The Evolution of Management Thought* (4th Ed.). New York: John Wiley & Sons.

NOTES

159

www.ingramcontent.com/pod-product-compliance
Lightning Source LLC
Chambersburg PA
CBHW031515270326
41930CB00006B/403